EARLY AMERICAN
WALL STENCILS
IN COLOR

Full-Size Patterns Traced in New England Homes and Stencils
from Early Coverlets, Together with
Complete Directions
Showing How Anyone Can Use Them with Ease

Alice Bancroft Fjelstul and Patricia Brown Schad
with
Barbara Marhoefer

BONANZA BOOKS
New York

This 1989 edition is published by Bonanza Books,
distributed by Crown Publishers, Inc., 225 Park Avenue South,
New York, New York 10003, by arrangement with E. P. Dutton,
a division of NAL Penguin, Inc.

Printed and Bound in Italy

Design: The Etheredges

Library of Congress Cataloging-in-Publication Data

Fjelstul, Alice Bancroft.
Early American wall stencils in color : full-size patterns traced in
New England homes and stencils from early coverlets, together with complete
directions showing how anyone can use them with ease / Alice Bancroft Fjelstul
and Patricia Brown Schad with Barbara Marhoefer
Reprint. Originally published: New York : Dutton, 1982.
Bibliography: p. Includes index.
ISBN 0-517-68239-7
1. Stencil work—New England. I. Schad, Patricia Brown.
II. Marhoefer, Barbara. III. Title.
[TT270.F44 1989]
745.7'3'0974—dc20
89-7067
CIP
ISBN 0-517-68239-7
h g f e d c b a

Our special thanks go to the owners of the private historic houses who welcomed us into their parlors to photograph and trace original patterns. Special thanks are also due Moses Eaton's great-grandchildren, Willard C. Richardson, Louisa Richardson Fairchild, and Robert E. Richardson, and Janet Waring's great-niece, Barbara Hunt Smith. We also thank the many interested people we corresponded with who are currently involved in research on wall stencils.

We gratefully acknowledge the following people who generously aided our research: Edith Prout, Jenkintown Library, Jenkintown, Pennsylvania; William Douglas, Franklin Pierce Homestead, Hillsboro, New Hampshire; Florence Flores, Amherst, New Hampshire; Laura Byers, Museum of American Folk Art, New York; Carolyn Ibbotson, Cortland County Historical Society, Cortland, New York; Ellen W. Mott, Cortland, New York; Jane E. Radcliffe, Maine State Museum, Augusta, Maine; Sandra S. Armentrout, Brick Store Museum, Kennebunk, Maine; and Dottie Hanson, Edina, Minnesota.

Extra special thanks go to our husbands and children who cheerfully supported this project and whose enthusiasm helped make this book possible.

Research for this book was funded in part by a grant from the National Endowment for the Arts.

CONTENTS

Chapter One: AN EARLY AMERICAN DECORATIVE FOLK ART   1

Chapter Two: AN ANCIENT TOOL DEVELOPED IN A SPECIAL YANKEE WAY   6

Chapter Three: MATERIALS   12

Chapter Four: STEP-BY-STEP COACHING   14

Chapter Five: CREATE A STENCILED ROOM   18

Chapter Six: STENCIL BEDSPREADS, CURTAINS, AND OTHER FABRICS   21

Chapter Seven: A GALLERY OF STENCIL DESIGNS   23

    Section 1: JOSIAH SAGE HOUSE, SOUTH SANDISFIELD, MASSACHUSETTS   23

    Section 2: HALL TAVERN, HISTORIC DEERFIELD, DEERFIELD, MASSACHUSETTS   36

    Section 3: PETER FARNUM HOMESTEAD, FRANCESTOWN, NEW HAMPSHIRE   42

    Section 4: FRANKLIN PIERCE HOMESTEAD, HILLSBORO, NEW HAMPSHIRE   46

    Section 5: KENNETH LEARY HOUSE, FARMINGTON, NEW HAMPSHIRE   49

    Section 6: STEPHEN DAMON HOUSE, AMHERST, NEW HAMPSHIRE   59

    Section 7: MID-EIGHTEENTH-CENTURY FARMHOUSE, DANVILLE, NEW HAMPSHIRE   66

    Section 8: TAYLOR-BARRY HOUSE, KENNEBUNK, MAINE   77

    Section 9: DAVID THOMPSON HOUSE, KENNEBUNK, MAINE   80

    Section 10: WATERMAN HOUSE, WALDOBORO, MAINE   89

Section 11: TOBIAS RICKER HOUSE, BUCKFIELD, MAINE   93

Section 12: WELCOME ROOD TAVERN AND J. W. HILL FARM, FOSTER, RHODE ISLAND   102

Section 13: BATTY-BARDEN HOUSE, SCITUATE, RHODE ISLAND   107

Section 14: SMITH-APPLEBY HOUSE, SMITHFIELD, RHODE ISLAND   111

Section 15: PATTERNS FROM TWO COVERLETS AND A TABLECLOTH   120

SUGGESTIONS FOR ALTERNATIVE COLOR SCHEMES   133

Chapter Eight: FOLLOWING THE TRAIL OF THE JOURNEYMAN STENCILER   134

NOTES   135

BIBLIOGRAPHY   136

AUTHORS' BIOGRAPHIES   138

INDEX   138

Chapter One

AN EARLY AMERICAN DECORATIVE FOLK ART

Strawberries . . . we saw a simple, woven basket full of lush berries in all their springtime glory stenciled over a bedroom mantel; it was our first look at early American stenciling.

We, Alice Fjelstul and Pat Schad, were in the bedroom of an 1815 farmhouse off a country road in Amherst, New Hampshire. We marveled at the green vine, thick with red strawberries, creeping along the baseboards and stenciled on walls covered with a raspberry wash. We admired the green and red leafy and geometric patterns and the green and red frieze of wildflowers near the ceiling. We had not been prepared for the astonishing beauty and bold color of an original stenciled room.

Our research up to that time had been conducted mostly with black-and-white photographs. We found that the designs were far bigger than we had expected and were closer together—often only six to twelve inches apart.

1. Moses Eaton's strawberry stenciling in the bedroom of the Stephen Damon House, Amherst, New Hampshire. Eaton improvised the basket of strawberries over the mantel. *(Photograph courtesy Horace A. Brown)*

The bedroom we were in was in the house Stephen Damon built when he married Nancy Fisk in 1815. The stenciler had painted just one willow tree in the room and had placed it prominently between the two front windows. The willow was the early American symbol for long life and immortality—this was the stenciler's gift to the couple.

Who was the stenciler?

We recognized the designs as being some of the documented patterns of Moses Eaton, Jr., the most prolific of the early stencilers; the patterns had been found in his old stencil kit. By using only two colors and balancing leafy floral and fruit designs with geometric motifs, Eaton had achieved a harmony and elegance that we were admiring 150 years later. We had not expected to find his work on the first stenciled walls we saw.

We were hooked.

After our first encounter that warm spring day we continued to search for examples of this wonderful decorative art. Any early authentic stenciled room we heard about, we wanted to see ourselves; someone else's description only whetted our eagerness. A photograph in a magazine or a letter from a stranger only added to our desire to see more wall stenciling.

This book brings you many of the best patterns we found and traced, so that you too can enjoy the work of the itinerant artists who created this important American folk art from 1800 through the 1840s.

The early stencilers traveled simply enough, with just their brushes, dry pigments, and a roll of stencils, which consisted of patterns cut in heavy paper. Often, to sell their talents, they would stencil a sampler of designs on an attic wall or in a closet for prospective customers to study. They took patterns from nature—leaves, wildflowers, vines, trees, birds, and stars. They asked for skimmed milk with which to make paint, and asked for their lodging and meals plus a small fee or some product from the farm or from the family in trade for their talents. They would stay for a week or longer, bringing the family news from afar, for they

2. Stenciler's sampler of designs on the attic wall, Josiah Sage House, South Sandisfield, Massachusetts. To sell his talents to the householders, the artist tested some of his designs here. His repertoire and colors, as seen throughout the house, proved far richer.

The stencil artists painted many popular Colonial symbols. The eagle, of course, represented pride in the new nation, and is often found with stars over its head indicating the number of states in the Union at the time the stenciling was done. The bell represented liberty and also happiness. In Bradford, New Hampshire, Moses Eaton stenciled a bedroom for a bride and groom with bells that had hearts for clappers.

The pineapple was a very popular symbol; it represented hospitality. In Maine many people on inland farms chose the pineapple for their walls, although it is likely that in the early 1800s they had never seen a real one. Perhaps they had heard that in Newport, Rhode Island, a famous Colonial seaport and the home of many ship captains, when a ship's master was safely home from the sea, he would place a pineapple over his doorway indicating that it was an open house with food and drink for all. Thus many Maine families, if they couldn't have a pineapple on their tables, had them adorning their walls. Moses Eaton stenciled pineapples in remote farmhouses in Maine that are still remote today.

often decorated inns, where they met people from distant towns.

First they painted the walls in an ochre (a mustard yellow) or gray or raspberry wash, and then stenciled them with patterns the family had selected in rich vivid colors—red, black, green, rust, and ochre. They painted friezes (deep borders) along the ceilings and narrower borders dropping vertically to the floors, or along chair rails, around doors and windows, and along the floors. They used these narrow borders to divide the walls into panels where they created central motifs, such as large flowers, sunbursts, willows, oak-leaf clusters, flowering sprays, and woven baskets containing flowers.

For a family with formal aspirations, they painted swags with bells and tassels in imitation of drapery gathered at two points, or columns that suggested the popular neo-classical style, or elegant urns containing flowers and ferns.

For a family that admired French wallpaper they covered the walls with allover patterns that were intricate and lacy and were applied with a precision that is astounding when you consider that they could not see through the stencil when applying the paint.

A family who chose designs with thistles, poppies, sunflowers, strawberries, pine cones, and leaves lived through the bitter winters surrounded by walls that promised summer's bounty and the fragrance of nearby forests.

The stencilers cut the patterns in heavy paper with knives, held the paper to the wall, and applied the paint through the design with a brush. For a three-color pattern they needed three stencils. If necessary, they improvised by cutting stencils on the spot, as Moses Eaton probably did when he created the basket of strawberries in the Amherst bedroom.

Stencils & brushes used by Moses Eaton

When a stenciler was finished, he left behind him walls blooming with color and design more alive and vibrant than wallpaper. Then off he traveled to stencil at the next farm or next village or even in the next state. Wall stenciling is found in New England, New York, and west to Ohio, even in Indiana and Texas.

Who were these artists?

They were mostly itinerant professionals plus some amateurs who worked as early as 1778, but most of their work was done between 1800 and 1840 before industrial progress brought cheap wallpaper and changes in tastes and styles. They were not artists who were academy-trained practi-

tioners of the fine arts for the rich and powerful. The stencilers were folk artists from the farms and villages and towns. Some were farmers who did their stenciling in the winter when they could leave their farms. They painted in cold, unheated rooms where the paint sometimes froze as it was applied to a wall.

They seldom signed a wall, so most of the artists are unknown today. The stencilers whose names are known number only fifteen, one woman and fourteen men, and very little else is known about most of them, except Moses Eaton, Jr.

Through a fortunate happenstance his kit, containing seventy-eight stencils, was discovered in the 1930s, so his work can be positively identified by matching the stencil to the painted motif. In addition, his family has supplied new information about him for this book.

Eaton learned stenciling from his father, Moses Eaton, Sr., who was also a professional stenciler. The younger Eaton traveled extensively, leaving his farm in Hancock, New Hampshire, and journeying north through New Hampshire and on into Maine. He hired men to help on his farm so he could travel. His patterns were big and bold; he had a fine feel for design and color; and his use of color was daring. His designs were copied by other stencilers.

Eaton was a creative artist with great vitality who turned to other pursuits when stenciling was no longer in style. He made wooden butter prints and furniture stencils; he wove linen from flax on a large loom and printed it with wooden blocks in leafy and floral designs, which he sold probably for use in embroidery.

What happened to the stenciled walls?

Many families enjoyed and treasured their stenciling for years, but as tastes changed, some papered, plastered, or painted over it. Some overmantels became so covered with soot that they were scrubbed, and the stenciling, usually the most elaborate patterns in the room, was worn off. Time was hard on some old plaster, which cracked and chipped, then it was replastered or destroyed, and thus some more stenciling was lost. As the decades passed many of the houses with stenciling were abandoned and fell into ruin or were destroyed. But the work of the stencilers was so pervasive that much stenciling remains today, either still exposed or hidden behind wallpaper and plaster.

Wall stenciling was also done in the late 1800s, some of it by Louis Comfort Tiffany, but Victorian stenciling was far different from early American work. The earlier work was considered quaint and naïve and was mostly unappreciated until the late 1920s. Then the real worth of American folk arts began to be recognized by artists and collectors, and authorities hailed the various folk arts as important products of the new American democracy, distinctive for a power, originality, and beauty that rivaled the academic arts.[1]

Not much was known at this time about early American stenciling, for no one had seriously collected and recorded the works until someone began the task in 1924.

That person was Janet Waring, an amateur furniture stenciler and prominent churchwoman from Yonkers, New York, who often spent summers in New England. Waring was the daughter of a wealthy hat manufacturer and a member of the Society of Mayflower Descendants. When she was around fifty, she casually began a long, scholarly study of stenciling that resulted in her landmark book, *Early American Stenciling on Walls and Furniture.*

Her book was published in 1937. Waring had worked thirteen years, traveling extensively in New England to trace patterns from walls and furniture. She went into quiet villages, up remote roads, into homes and abandoned houses falling into ruin, tracing patterns everywhere. She talked farmers into pulling hay out of old buildings, now hay barns, so she could trace the stenciling on the walls; then she paid them to put the hay back.[2] Because she did not drive, she was accompanied on these expeditions by her chauffeur, who often helped her pry off wallpaper and plaster.[3] On most of these expeditions Waring was accompanied by her sister, Susan B. Waring, who waited patiently in the car.

Janet Waring visited Moses Eaton's family year after year and they became friends. She learned that his stencil box was upstairs in their attic, probably just where he had set it years before.

In New England over that period of thirteen years she recorded wall stenciling from approximately eighty houses for her book, and more stencil patterns from furniture. Her avocation had grown into the major interest of her life. Her book was the only one on the subject for many years.

On the occasion of our Bicentennial in 1976 interest in stenciling grew in all sections of this country, and it was being used again as a method of decoration. More and more early American stenciling was being discovered and preserved in New England.

As a Bicentennial project we, Alice Fjelstul and Patricia Schad, funded by a grant from the National Endowment for the Arts, began to compile a collection of tracings of original designs before they were lost, faded, or destroyed. Many of the houses Janet Waring had recorded in her book are now gone. We found some, however, and searched out many more. We found the material in private homes and in such out-of-the-way places as in a closet at the top of a flight of stairs in a former tavern, now a used-furniture shop in Southwick, Massachusetts. We saw more patterns in historical societies and other associations, which had kept tracings of wall stencil designs from walls that had been destroyed.

Armed with our authentic designs we learned to stencil walls and fabrics. We devised our own methods using

twentieth-century materials. Because the early stencilers' materials were crude and difficult to use, we bypassed many of their practices (especially carrying their pigments in mouse and rat bladders!) and turned to such modern materials as clear vinyl plastic, masking tape, and latex paint.

We do not use oil-base paints, which can give a too-heavy look to stenciling, are slow drying, and make cleaning up a tedious chore. Latex and acrylic paints come very close to the light "thin" opaque look of the old milk paints. They are a joy to use; both latex and acrylic paints are water-soluble, easy to clean up after, and permanent when dry. Our stenciling techniques are quick, easy, and inexpensive, and we have taught them to many people.

The fruits of our work, both the collection of original patterns and complete instructions on how to apply them to your walls and fabrics, are to be found in this book. Armed with a few items from your neighborhood hardware, hobby, and variety stores, you are ready to begin.

INCLUDED IN THIS BOOK ARE:

► *More than seventy full-size early American patterns for stenciling walls and fabrics.* We traced the original patterns, cut stencils from them, and stenciled them on special paper for reproduction in this book in order to give you the proper texture and "feel" of this early American decorative art.

► *Patterns from early American stenciled coverlets and from a tablecloth.*

► *A page of alternative color schemes to provide variety in your decoration.*

► *Step-by-step directions for stenciling walls and fabrics.* You work right from this book with clear vinyl, permanent marking pens, a hobby knife, stout brushes, and latex paints.

► *The technique peculiar to stenciling.* The paint is not applied from the side of the brush as in fine arts painting; it is applied with the tips of the bristles and pounced or pounded onto the wall in firm strokes.

► *The early American fudge factor.* In our study of stenciling we have seen how the early artists *fudged* at the corners and over doorways: they used an extra element of the design or changed the spacing to turn the corner. They were not hampered by precise measuring.

► *Tips on how to decorate a home, office, or shop with stenciling.* These patterns will brighten a small room, tie together a difficult corner or stair wall, decorate a kitchen soffet, and pick up a design from your curtains.

► *How to cut a stencil from any pattern.* Directions that show how to use any design for stenciling, from your curtains, Oriental rugs, monogram, or club insignia.

► *List of places to see original designs.* There are quite a few places in New England where the public can see authentic early American stenciling.

► *The story of how the stencil developed in America.* This chapter will list fifteen wall stencilers.

Proclaim liberty unto all the inhabitants thereof

We have attempted to answer all your questions about early American stenciling, for at our workshops and lectures we have met hundreds of people interested in this folk art. After more than a century wall stenciling is being recognized for what it is—an important part of our artistic heritage that is threatened by time and ignorance. This book preserves many of the old patterns and places them in your hands to help you create something in your environment that will be unique. You will find that stenciling is fun, has a classic simplicity, and gives quick fulfillment.

Happy stenciling!

Chapter Two

AN ANCIENT TOOL DEVELOPED IN
A SPECIAL YANKEE WAY

A king used a stencil to sign his name. Theodoric the Great, king of the Ostrogoths, traced the first four letters of his name through a stencil cut in a gold plate in the sixth century in Italy.

In medieval Europe craftsmen used stencils to decorate playing cards and religious prints, which often were the only bits of brightness in the somber homes of the lower classes.

Later the French used stencils to make flocked paper, elegant wallpaper with designs created with ground velvet or wool. The patterns were stenciled in glue and then dusted with velvet or wool powder, giving the paper a texture suggesting brocade.

The word *stencil* is itself French. It is derived from the old French word *estenceler,* which means "to cover with sparkle," and which is itself derived from the Latin word *scintilla,* which means a "spark."

Stenciling was, as a French scholar wrote in 1888, a "process known to everyone, and as old as the need to which it responds."[1]

The stencil is a humble tool and a very ancient one. It is simply a cutout pattern through which one or more colors are applied to a surface. It is a process that has been used for many centuries. In the fifth century B.C. the Etruscans decorated their magnificent vases with stencils—patterns cut into sheets of very thin copper, which could be bent any way.[2]

Many centuries later other artisans stenciled fabrics in the Fiji Islands in the South Pacific, in Japan, and in Western Nigeria. In Fiji women stenciled wide geometric patterns cut into banana leaves in black on bark cloth or on masi, which was used as mosquito netting.[3] In Japan artisans cut intricate designs in mulberry paper and stenciled in many colors on silk and cotton for Nō robes, which were stage costumes, for futons (mattresses for sleeping), and for kimonos.[4] In Western Nigeria, Yoruba artists, when making adire cloth for garments, used indigo dye and stencils cut into thin sheet iron or zinc to create geometric designs on cotton.[5]

Here in the United States perhaps the earliest printed reference to the use of a stencil was a newspaper advertisement in 1796: William Priest advertised in a Baltimore newspaper for his "Painting In imitation of Paperhangings, By a mechanical process" that was far cheaper but just as beautiful as wallpaper. The advertisement read:

> Priest, William, Painter, Interior Work, Painting In imitation of Paperhangings, By a mechanical process, which, from its facility, enables the artist to paint a room, staircase, &c. upon lower terms, than it is possible to hang with paper of equal beauty . . . He offers his services as above or in laying plain grounds in distemper with plain or festoon borders.[6]

But Priest was not the only early stenciler. His advertisement appeared eighteen years after stenciling was done in Marlborough, Massachusetts, which was the earliest stenciling that Janet Waring found.

That stenciling was done in 1778, two years after the signing of the Declaration of Independence, for Abner Goodale, who was at home recuperating from wounds he had suffered at the Battle of White Plains. Goodale was engaged to marry Molly Howe of Sudbury, two miles away, and he had his house enlarged and (in Colonial terms) "redded up" for his bride. He had five new rooms stenciled, one of which must have been his bedroom, for it was stenciled with a frieze of swags and bells—wedding bells.[7]

Most stenciling was done after 1800, when increasing prosperity resulted in more and larger houses. People yearned for color and decoration in their lives. They began to employ stencilers and other artists who traveled the turnpikes and back roads with the other itinerants of the times: peddlers, tinkers, preachers, weavers, tailors, candlemakers, and men who painted the exteriors of houses, barns, and outbuildings.

The artists included portrait painters, sign and mural painters, silhouette cutters, and decorators of bridal chests

and other furniture, fireboards, and ordinary household utensils. Many traveled great distances.

Rufus Porter of West Boxford, Massachusetts, was a portrait and mural painter who used stenciling; in 1819 and 1820 he traveled on foot from Boston to Hot Springs, Virginia. Earlier he had sailed to the American Northwest and Hawaii, where he paid his expenses by painting.[8]

Moses Eaton's usual stenciling trips were in a northeasterly direction. He left his farm in the lower southwest corner of New Hampshire and traveled up through his state into Maine. His patterns are found frequently in Maine, beginning in Eliot, one of the first towns over the border near the coast, then along the coast through Kennebunk, Portland, North Saco (inland at Buckfield), Waldoboro, Hope, and further north to the Blue Hill area, which is near Bar Harbor and Acadia National Park, and also inland and north to Sebec, which is almost at the central point of the state.

Did Eaton ever travel west of New Hampshire? Surely, such an adventurous artistic spirit as he thought about going west, a new area in those times where land was opening up for settlement. A member of Eaton's family recalled that Eaton said he took a trip "west to Ohio," but he did not say if he did stenciling there.[9]

Some Eaton-like patterns have been found in central New York and along routes leading west to Ohio that were popular in the first half of the nineteenth century. Leigh Rehner Jones found these patterns while doing research for her thesis on decorative wall painting. The patterns found include Eaton's favorites: the oak-leaf cluster, oak-leaf frieze, flower basket, willow and diamond, and vertical leaf border.[10]

"These motifs," she wrote in her thesis, "can be followed like a ghostly Johnny Appleseed's apple trees from the New England states west through New York and into Ohio and Indiana."[11]

In our research we discovered that some groups of patterns were repeated in specific areas, suggesting that some stencilers worked in individual regions. For example, we saw the border stencil patterns found in the Franklin Pierce Homestead, Hillsboro, New Hampshire, again in the Peterborough area, about ten miles to the southwest. (We suspect that this stenciler, now referred to as the "border stenciler," took a trip to Maine, for we found the same patterns in the Taylor-Barry House in Kennebunk. See stencils 39 and 40.)

Another group of patterns found at the western edge of Rhode Island near Foster are very similar to those found just over the border in Connecticut.

3. Watercolor of Mrs. Rebecca Jaques, Poseyville, Indiana, by Dr. Jacob Maentel, 1841. When Mrs. Jaques sat for her portrait in southwest Indiana, she posed in front of a stenciled wall in her parlor. *(Photograph courtesy Abby Aldrich Rockefeller Folk Art Center, Williamsburg, Virginia)*

Still another group of patterns are typical of the area around Smithfield, Rhode Island, which is near Providence at the eastern edge of the state. (See stencils 61–67.)

Some patterns are far-flung indeed. Patterns from the Josiah Sage House in South Sandisfield, Massachusetts, are found across New York State in the Rochester area, about 250 miles away. A crude rendering of a border from the same Josiah Sage House was found more than 600 miles to the west, near McConnelsville, Ohio, about 20 miles south of Zanesville.[12]

Of course, no stenciler could boast of having exclusive designs. There was no copyright to protect them, and because public places such as inns and meeting halls were often stenciled, many patterns were copied freehand or even traced by other craftsmen.

Lydia Eldredge Williams, the only known woman stenciler, used many original patterns in the two rooms she stenciled in her home in Ashfield Massachusetts, particularly the red flames rising from little piles of firewood. But perhaps there is a connection between the black tulip she used in a bedroom and a black tulip—identical in size and design—dimly seen on a bedroom floor in the Wayside Inn at Sudbury, about eighty miles away. Did Mrs. Williams stencil the inn's floor? Or did she trace the tulip one night when she stayed there? Or did someone, knowing her artistic talents, trace it for her?

Although stenciling may be common in an area, the names of the stencilers are usually unknown. In Blue Hill, Maine, and the immediate surrounding area there is a good deal of very fine stenciling. Dorothy H. Candage, who has been studying stenciling there for almost twenty years, wrote that she "looked through many old papers, but have never been able to find any mention of even one itinerant painter in Blue Hill." [13]

There is, however, an extraordinary amount of information about Moses Eaton, Jr. His work is easily identified because seventy-eight of his stencils were found in his old stencil kit. He is the best known of the early stencilers and undoubtedly the most popular because of his big, bold, imaginative work, his vivid colors, and his feel for design and color.

Eaton, the son of a farmer and stenciler, Moses Eaton, Sr., was born in the White Mountains of New Hampshire on August 3, 1796, in Hancock, a small town in the southwest corner of the state between Peterborough and Keene. The family was descended from people who had settled Dedham, Massachusetts, and the senior Eaton had fought in the Revolution.

The younger Eaton learned stenciling from his father and when he was old enough to travel (he was eighteen in 1814), he was already an accomplished stenciler. When not traveling, he lived with his father and mother, Esther Ware Eaton, on their farm in Hancock.

When he arrived in a remote village, he carried a small and modest outfit to ply his craft: a wooden stencil box containing dry colors, round stout brushes, measuring tools, and a roll of stencils, cut into thick paper. He visited various households and put a variety of patterns on walls in attics or inside closets from which the householders could select. In addition to stenciling he offered to paint their white plaster walls in soft shades of ochre, raspberry, or gray wash that allowed the features and flaws of the plaster to show through.

When Eaton went to work, he was probably efficient and worked neatly—his old stencils were found without paint on the underside. His stenciling was opaque and flat, never shaded. He used dark green (a favorite color), red, black, yellow, and rose.

Eaton's work was not the work of a trained artist, but that of a farmer with a sense of color and design. Occasionally, he stenciled designs off center and in corners he fudged to make them fit. Some stencilers imitated French wallpaper with delicate intricate lacy designs and many small patterns, but Eaton did not; he did not try to be fancy and probably had never seen French wallpaper.

His father was still stenciling occasionally, and family tradition says they used the same stencils. It is hard to be sure which Eaton did what stenciling, but it is generally agreed that Eaton, Sr., stenciled some houses in Hancock and the immediate area, and that his son did too, as well as traveling in New Hampshire and Maine. Eaton, Sr., was forty-three when his son was born, and was sixty-one when he was eighteen in 1814, the age many young men leave home. It is most likely that the father did not travel very far from Hancock during the following years when wall stenciling was flourishing, for he was in his late sixties and early seventies, and travel was difficult in those days.

When Moses Eaton, Jr., was twenty-eight in 1824, another young itinerant artist came to Hancock—Rufus Porter, who was four years his senior and primarily a mural painter.[14] Porter and the Eatons became friends, and he worked with the younger man on several houses in Hancock and one in Bradford, about twenty miles to the north, which was owned by Joshua Eaton.

When working in a bedroom in this house, Moses Eaton showed he was not hampered by careful calculations. When he discovered that his frieze would not fit over a door, he changed to a narrower border, used it over the door, and resumed the larger design on the other side. As he approached a corner, he discovered that he had a space to fill that would not take the beginning of a new pattern; so he simply repeated a swag close to an identical one, and continued stenciling.

Eaton and Porter traveled together on a painting trip, and eventually worked in Sebec, Maine. At a house there Porter did spongework painting (that is, applying paint with a sponge), filling out Eaton's trees and creating bases for his woven flower baskets. Porter also painted landscapes with spongework trees and a repeated figure of a groom holding an unsaddled horse, which was a stencil.[15]

We think we have found another house where they worked together about eighty miles southwest of Sebec in Buckfield, Maine. It is the Tobias Ricker House, a simple farmhouse high on a hill. The patterns are Moses Eaton's, but they are changed and elaborated; the stenciling has some of the most colorful and complicated work we have seen. It includes a pineapple rendered in four colors, a motif that usually appears in only two colors. The fruit is ochre with a touch of cadmium red on top and has leaves in two shades of green—olive and a darker and bluer green. We found freehand painting and spongework under the willow trees—touches of Rufus Porter. (See stencils 49–53.)

What was a stenciler or mural painter paid? Porter, writing twenty-two years after he and Eaton traveled together, said that $10 was the usual fee for painting a room with landscape frescoes, and this may also have been the stenciling fee.[16] Porter went his way, filling walls with his robust, gay, unpretentious murals that celebrated the beauties of the coast and countryside.

When not traveling, Eaton continued to live at his father's farm. Moses Eaton, Sr., died in 1833 when he was eighty, and his son was thirty-seven. Two years later Moses Eaton married Rebecca Platt of Dublin, New Hampshire, a nearby town, and they settled on a farm in Harrisville, which was part of the town of Hancock. They had three children, a boy and two girls: Luther, born 1836, Mary, born 1838, and Sarah, born 1840.

Moses Eaton took pride in his farming. According to the family, his corn was the best in the area. He had a fine herd of registered Devon cattle, triple-purpose animals that gave milk and meat and functioned as beasts of burden. He also raised Blue Hen chickens, which were reputed to breed fierce gamecocks.

Some scholars believe that Moses Eaton gave up stenciling and traveling after he married, but his family states that he continued to travel and stencil for many years after his marriage. Eaton's daughter, Mary, often told her grandchildren that her family had a "rather hard time managing at home on the farm with her father gone so much of the time. Of course, they had hired hands, but it was very difficult with the man of the house always away."[17]

Eaton's younger daughter, Sarah, died when she was eighteen, and his son Luther never married. His only descendants are through Mary, who married Luke Richardson and lived on a farm in nearby Dublin. When Moses Eaton was older, he and his wife, Rebecca, gave up their farm and moved to Dublin to live with Mary and her family.

He stenciled the front parlor in Mary's house, and years later in the 1930s when Janet Waring visited that house, the Richardsons who lived there told her about the stenciling hidden under the wallpaper. It had been discovered in 1918 when the wallpaper was peeled off and Mary was present. The sight of her father's work had brought back a flood of memories.

4. Moses Eaton, Jr., around 1860 when he was sixty-four. *(Photograph courtesy Shelburne Museum, Shelburne, Vermont; Gift of the Family)*

Janet Waring visited the house once a year and became good friends with the Richardsons. On her fifth visit she found that they were going to redecorate: they were consulting a wallpaper sample book. Because of Waring's interest they stripped off the old paper, so she could see the patterns Moses Eaton had chosen.

He had painted the walls a soft raspberry and had stenciled patterns in deep green and red. Between the two front windows he had created a large woven basket filled with flowers. Around the four walls next to the ceiling he had stenciled a frieze of swags and bells. Along the baseboard and again over the chair rail there was a strawberry border. The walls between the chair rails and the ceiling were divided into nineteen-inch panels by his favorite diamond leaf vertical border. Inside these panels Eaton had made green and red geometric central designs alternating with flowers with large red centers.[18] (See stencils 28–32.)

The Richardsons told Waring that Eaton's old stencil box was tucked away in the attic, and it eventually came into her possession. She studied it and said it made her feel "almost a partaker in his day's work."[19] She found it contained eight worn brushes and seventy-eight stencils that made up into forty complete designs. There were no register marks on the stencils, indicating that for accurate placing of a stencil on a design already painted on a wall, Eaton depended on his judgment and the upper edge of the stencil.

In addition, she found in the kit small woodblocks with designs cut on two sides: circles, wreaths, flower petals, vines, and stars, some still showing traces of green paint. Moses Eaton used them to stamp fabric, such as the linen he wove on his large loom.[20] He sold this fabric, cut into small pieces, probably for use in embroidery.

After Eaton gave up his farm, he recorded this and other methods of earning money in a diary that is now in the possession of his family. He wrote that he worked neighbors' fields with a team of oxen. He made shoes and wooden butter prints with strawberry and wheat designs. He also made brass stencils, which he used to paint the sides of cupboards and other furniture. The family owns one of these stencils, a cat design. Moses Eaton wrote that for all these types of work he earned 10¢ an hour. He did not mention wall stenciling in this diary.[21] Eaton died in Dublin, November 16, 1886, when he was ninety years old.

Janet Waring treasured his stencil box, and after her death her sister donated it to The Society for the Preservation of New England Antiquities in Boston.

Most of Eaton's stencils are included in this book in their actual size.

Early American paints and pigments. Early American wall stenciling achieved its distinctive originality and beauty with crude materials that were difficult to use and were often homemade.

Stencilers cut their patterns in heavy brown paper, similar to oaktag, which was oiled or covered with animal fat to keep the paint from penetrating it. A few stencilers used leather, which is extremely difficult to cut.

Stencilers made their paint from skimmed milk, adding lime, oil, and whiting, which was pure white chalk ground very fine; to this paint they added dry pigments for color. A thrifty stenciler tried to make as many pigments as he could, and there were many old recipes available in the early 1800s.

Red was made from boiling iron filings or from brick dust or from the juice of pokeweed berries, which was called the "red ink plant" and grew commonly by the roadside.

Black was obtained from lampblack, which was a finely powdered black soot deposited from smoke or a smoky flame onto the glass chimney of a lamp; Rufus Porter said he mixed it with rum or water. Another black was made from burning nutshells in an iron pan, then grinding them on marble with oil or varnish.

5. Heavy paper stencils in the collection of Old Sturbridge Village, Sturbridge, Massachusetts. About 150 years ago an unidentified stenciler cut and used these patterns; they are still caked with paint.

Yellow was obtained from clays found in the earth. A yellowish green, considered yellow, was made from "French berries," the berries of the ripe buckthorn.

Clays may also have supplied gray-green and plum pigments. Rufus Porter painted murals in grays and greens in a group of houses in eastern Massachusetts, and these murals might well have had clay-based pigments. There are gray-green and plum clay stones washed up on the beaches nearby in Massachusetts, and there is plum-colored clay in the ground.[22]

Blue was difficult to obtain from nature in New England. The indigo plant, a good source, did not grow in that cold climate. One old recipe for blue called for boiling the blue leaves of a "large quantity of blowart, which grows in the fields among the corn." "Blowart" was probably the cornflower, which had a long-stemmed blue head with florets that yielded a blue juice, which was used as a dye.

Most professional stencilers, however, purchased their pigments in color shops and in glaziers' shops. Many of those shops were using steam engines to grind pigments in the early 1800s; this brought the price down and also increased the supply.

A stenciler in a rural area could order from these shops by mail or through friends or relatives in the cities or through city merchants who acted as brokers. Joseph Dickinson, who owned a wallpaper and color shop in Philadelphia, advertised that he specialized in "trading to any part of America." In an advertisement printed June 30, 1786, in the *Pennsylvania Packet,* he wrote: "Country orders punctually executed. Paper money taken. Likewise, Allum [*sic*], Indigo, best Tobacco, and Produce at their current prices."[23] (Alum was aluminum potassium sulfate, which was used in barter.)

In addition, stencilers could buy commercially produced

pigments from stores in towns or from country stores or, of course, from the peripatetic Yankee peddlers.

For some peddlers the selling of indigo, other dyes, and pigments actually became a specialty; the indigo peddler was a familiar salesman even before the Revolution. Indigo plants were cultivated in the South at that time and indigo was a profitable crop; after the Revolution much indigo was imported from the East Indies, where it was raised more cheaply than in the South.[24]

The color shops used some formulas for green pigment that called for verdigris, which was a green rust on copper, and might have been obtained by the action of dilute acetic acid on sheet copper. In our research we found some stenciling that we suspected was once green but had faded into yellow-green, probably because the verdigris pigment broke down after time on the walls, as in the Josiah Sage House.

People have asked if the Pennsylvania Germans stenciled the walls in their homes; the question is suggested by the rich, colorful designs painted on their furniture. We have searched for wall stenciling in the Pennsylvania German countryside and have found only isolated cases of stenciling, never the trail of patterns we found in New England.

OTHER WALL STENCILERS

Henry O. Goodrich—*Buried in Nottingham, New Hampshire.*

Emery Rice—*From Hancock, New Hampshire.*

Nathaniel Parker—*Worked in North Weare, New Hampshire.*

An artist who signed his name "Stimp" worked in Washington, Connecticut, and Dover Plains, New York.

Erastus Gates—*Worked in Plymouth, Vermont.*

J. H. De Forest—*From Pittsfield, Massachusetts.*

An artist who signed his name "Leroy" worked in western New York near Rochester.

Irwin DeWitt Baldwin—*From Van Deusen (vicinity of Great Barrington), Massachusetts.*

E. J. Gilbert—*Student and nephew of Rufus Porter*

Jonathan D. Poor—*Student of Rufus Porter*

These ten, plus those mentioned in this chapter—Moses Eaton, Sr., and, Jr., Rufus Porter, Lydia Eldredge Williams, and William Priest—bring the number of known stencilers to fifteen.

Chapter Three

MATERIALS

Stenciling with our method is easy and inexpensive; you work right from this book and need only a few materials, all of which are readily available from your hardware, paint, hobby, and variety stores. Don't let an art store sell you stencil paper, architect's linen, or Japan paints, which are materials other stencilers use—you won't need them. They are difficult and time-consuming to use.

1. Stencils. Cut your patterns out of clear vinyl plastic, sold in variety and fabric stores for approximately $3.00 per yard. In variety stores it is usually kept in the household department along with vinyl shelf paper and oilcloth. Buy heavy ten- or twelve-gauge vinyl. You need one-half yard.

2. Cutting tools. At a hardware, art, or hobby shop buy a small, sharp hobby knife that has a slim handle, which allows you to cut as you hold it like a pencil. Buy an X-acto No. 1 handle and a package of No. 10 curved blades. Another good brand is PO Precision Tools; you need that company's No. 111 knife and No. 10 curved blades.

Remove the straight blade the knife comes equipped with and insert the curved blade, which is better for cutting flexible plastic. To change the blade of either brand simply release the original blade by twisting the knife handle just below the blade *counterclockwise.* Pull out the straight blade (be careful of the cutting edge!), insert the curved blade, and then twist the handle in a *clockwise* direction to lock the blade in.

X-acto knife
with a No. 10 curved blade

3. Brushes. From a paint store buy two round, sash paintbrushes with *natural* bristles, often called "Chinese bristles." The bristle content of a brush is printed on the handle. Don't buy artificial bristles, such as nylon, because they don't hold the paint well. A No. 6 sash brush is good to start with; buy one for each color you intend to use. A No. 8 brush is good for larger patterns. A sash brush with natural bristles costs roughly from $2.50 to $4.50, depending on size. If you can't get round sash brushes, your art store or paint store can order large stencil brushes, which are more expensive.

4. Paint. Use latex paint, the great modern invention that washes up easily with soap and water. You can stencil with latex paint directly from the can. You can also use artists' acrylic paints, which come in tubes or small plastic jars. They are good for small accent colors, such as berries or flower centers. If you wish to alter a color, you can mix artists' acrylic paints with latex paints because the bases are the same. To lighten a color, add white; to darken one, add black or brown.

To match the colors in this book, take the book to a paint store or get sample "paint chips" from the store before you buy the paint. Most paint manufacturers have developed many fine Colonial colors since the Bicentennial. If buying a custom color, have it mixed as a *flat-finish* latex. You will not need more than a pint of each color.

5. Two permanent markers. For tracing your pattern on the vinyl, you need two differently colored *permanent* markers with narrow tips, such as laundry markers. They must be *permanent,* otherwise your lines will wear off as you cut your stencil and scrub it later on. We use laundry markers, and their marks last and last, even after repeated scrubbings.

If you can't find two differently colored permanent markers (black is easy to find), you can use just one color and indicate the areas to cut for your second color by shading in with diagonal lines or by using dotted lines to outline the second color.

6. *Plus a few household items.* You have the remaining necessary materials around your home.

a) For a palette save your meat trays from the supermarket. These light styrofoam trays are easy to clean of meat traces and they are ideal for holding paint. You can also use paper plates or plastic-container tops. Mix your paints on these homemade palettes, which are easy to carry up a ladder. You need a palette for each color to be used.

b) Masking tape—three-fourths-inch to one-inch width.

c) For a cutting surface you need a pad of newspapers, a piece of glass, cardboard, or what we use—a piece of vinyl floor tile.

d) Paper on which to practice stenciling. We use newsprint, which is sold in tablets in art stores and is inexpensive.

e) Old newspapers, rags, paper towels, and warm, soapy water.

f) Plastic scouring pads, such as the dark green Scotch-Brite Scouring Pads from the 3M Company.

ADDITIONAL ITEMS YOU'LL NEED

1. A stepladder.
2. A plumb line (string and a piece of chalk) or a level, plus a yardstick.
3. Lots of masking tape. If you're working on old plaster, use draftsman's tape instead, it doesn't grip as strongly.
4. Newspapers for the floor and for cleaning stencils.
5. Wet rags and a pail of warm, sudsy water.

Now, before you begin, wrap your paintbrushes with masking tape to hold the bristles rigid. It is important to work with stiff bristles. Starting at the base of the bristles, wrap the tape around and around until only about one-half inch of the bristles shows. The wrapping holds them firm as you pound the paint on the wall.

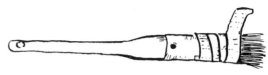

Sash brush wrapped with masking tape

TIPS ON COLORS

► To make any color, even a raw yellow, seem old, tone it down with raw umber, an artists' acrylic paint, available in small tubes at art stores.

► Wet paint in the can is not the same color after the paint has dried. Therefore, paint swatches of the color on paper, tape it to the walls and study it in different lights. One family that had stenciling done in the dining room—vines with clusters of grayish-pink berries—discovered that the berries *disappeared* in candlelight!

► Use colors that are dark enough to show the complete design. The early stencilers often painted the fruit part of their pineapples in red because yellow was too pale.

Chapter Four

STEP-BY-STEP COACHING

You've assembled your materials, so now begin. You can work easily on a kitchen table.

1. Pick your pattern. In this book you will find a variety of patterns that can be classified as large motifs we call *central units* (such as the pineapple, flower baskets, flower sprays); *borders* (narrow bands including strawberry, leaf, and floral patterns); and *friezes* (deep ornamental bands usually used along ceilings, such as the oak-leaf frieze). For your first stencil, pick a border or a simple frieze. Choose a one- or two-color pattern. Don't choose one with small dots because it's hard to cut dots at first, and with a few stencils behind you, they will come more easily.

2. Trace the complete design on two pieces of vinyl. For a two-color pattern, for example green and red, you need two different stencils, one for the green part and one for the red. Cut the green parts of the design on the first stencil and the red parts on the second. You will need to trace the *complete* design on *both* to help you line it up on the wall. We call these *register marks*.

Cut two rectangular pieces of vinyl the size of the patterns and include a one-inch border all around the pattern. For a border pattern leave about four inches at each end

for the repeat. Lay your first piece of vinyl over the pattern in this book and trace the green portion of the design in one color marker and the red portion in the second color. Repeat this process on your second piece of vinyl. If you're doing a border or a frieze, trace the beginning of a pattern repeat at each end to help you line up the design on the wall, but do *not* cut out these pattern repeats.

Before you have finished tracing, write "This Side Up" or "Top" in big letters on the *front top* of both stencils. This is very important, so that you don't apply the stencil upside down or backward.

When your two stencils are laid one over the other, they should give you the complete original pattern.

3. Cut out the pattern. Hold the knife as you would a pencil only with a bit more pressure. Use the curved cutting edge of your blade. Cut in long, sweeping, positive strokes. Turn the stencil with your other hand as you cut, which helps give a more fluid motion to the process.

Cut out the green part of the design on the first stencil and the red part on the second. Start cutting on a minor part of the design. If you are hesitant about cutting a leaf, trace it on an extra piece of vinyl and practice cutting it there.

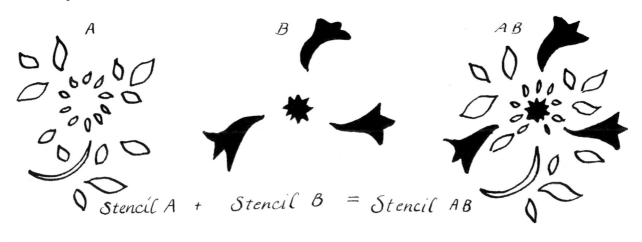

Stencil A + Stencil B = Stencil AB

Zigzag leaves are a bit tricky. Cut from the *outside* of the pattern toward the *center*. You are going to remove the vinyl inside, so it doesn't matter how many slices are in the inside piece. Punch out these pieces as you proceed.

Beginners often use short, halting strokes and always worry when they go out of a line. Don't stop your stroke if you do this, but try to continue and *cut* back to the line. Nobody is going to hold you to staying in the lines. Just keep cutting; the pattern becomes your own this way.

If your blade slips and you make too large a cut, simply mend the accidental cut with masking tape.

When you have finished cutting, lay one stencil over the other to be sure you have cut the entire design.

cut into the center

4. *Mix paint on your palette.* You will need only a tiny bit of paint. If you are squeezing it from a tube, you need a dab of paint the size of a few green peas. Take your brush and using the *end* of the bristles (not the side as in fine art painting), smear the paint around a bit.

This is a good place to point out the *big mistake* beginners make—using too much paint! Their first stenciling is usually terribly heavy and dark. This gives the wrong look to the stenciling; it should be rather soft, light, and have an almost powdery effect from up close. *Never* go back over your stenciling to try to fill in.

5. *Practice stenciling on paper.* The stenciling stroke is a pounding one, using the *flat end* of the wrapped bristles of your brush and holding it like a potato masher. Put a small amount of paint on the end of your brush and *pounce* on newspaper until there is very little paint left.

Use the stencil for the predominant color first. Holding the stencil down with one hand so it doesn't slip, pound your brush on newspaper to make sure you don't have too much paint on it, then move across the stencil, pounding the paint through the holes until your brush begins to run out of paint. When this happens, redip your brush and pounce off the excess on newspaper again before you resume stenciling. You may make as many as twenty practice

strokes before each application of paint through the pattern holes. Don't lift your stencil until you've finished applying paint to all the holes.

We really *pound* the paint against the stencil and the wall! This keeps the paint from smearing and getting under the stencil. We grip the brush in a fist and pound so hard that you can hear it in the next room.

When you have finished the first color, carefully lift your stencil and look at your work. If you had trouble getting the stencil up without smearing the design, you used too much paint. If the paint runs under the stencil when you lift it up, again you used too much. If the design is very dark and heavy, you used too much paint. If you are not sure, start again and this time use less paint. If you end up with a soft, powdery feeling, like the designs in this book, you have it right.

Beginners try to control the amount of paint by pounding lightly and this is wrong. Your pounding stroke should be standard—heavy all the time. Control the amount of paint by getting rid of the excess before starting to stencil.

To see the design come to life, stencil on the second color. You can do this right away because latex paints dry very quickly. Remember to use your *second* brush.

Practice for a short time, doing the complete design again. When you get the idea of the proper amount of paint . . .

6. *Practice stenciling on paper on a wall.* Attach some paper to a wall with masking tape. Now put your first stencil on the paper, held up with two pieces of masking tape at the top edge. Stencil your complete design on the paper, holding the bottom of the stencil steady with your free hand. This will give you a feeling of how hard to pound on a vertical surface.

7. *Clean as you go.* Clean your stencils as you work, probably every fifteen minutes or when they have built-up paint. As this paint is water soluble, just scrub off the excess with a soapy rag or a plastic scouring pad. Don't use steel wool because it rusts and breaks into little pieces. Remember, *never* let paint get on the undersides of your stencils. Clean the undersides occasionally as you work.

8. *Practice a sampler.* You are now so delighted with your pattern that you want to try it on a wall. Find an inconspicuous wall—a basement plasterboard wall, a closet, one you will paint over in the near future, or even an attic wall, just as the early stencilers used to do. Now stencil your design; if it is a frieze or a border, repeat it again and again.

Cut stencils for a central unit and practice it here too. Step back and you will see the soft, light feeling of period stenciling.

Begin to plan for a whole room. Cut stencils and *practice* the patterns you like in this book. Keep them taped up to

see the effect. You will need several central units, a frieze, and two borders.

9. *Have you made a mistake?* Correct mistakes immediately by wiping them off the wall with a wet rag, and re-stencil. Don't worry about imperfections; after all, they make it your own work. As you step away, small imperfections just melt into the whole beautiful effect.

10. *Cutting small holes.* Cutting small round holes is easy once you understand the method; here's how:

a) Trace several rows of small holes on a practice piece of vinyl. If you have a leather punch, you're probably itching to use it, so punch out a row of circles. It is almost as easy to cut each hole by hand and once you get used to it, it will be almost as fast.

b) Find a hard surface to cut against, such as the top side of a vinyl floor tile or glass.

c) Begin to cut the holes with your knife, sliding the stencil in one direction as you cut and moving the knife blade in the other. You will move along quickly if you make the *stencil* do most of the moving and let the blade move just a little. Now you can cut holes as small or as large as the pattern demands and you will get the rich variety of the old design.

11. *Practice stenciling a corner.* The early stencilers were not hampered by careful calculations and many did not measure out their designs, so they seldom turned a corner precisely where one design ended. They

a) stopped in mid-design and started it anew on the other wall;

b) just kept stenciling, leaving a partial design on one wall that was continued on the next wall (our vinyl stencils bend around corners);

c) repeated part of the design to fill in space on the first wall and started the pattern again on the second wall, for example, repeated a swag in the swag-and-bell frieze or a leaf in the acorn border;

d) changed the spacing before the corner, so the design ended at the corner.

You can do any of these things. We call it the Early American Fudge Factor. Don't worry about a perfect match; you are not trying to imitate wallpaper. Remember that the eye plays tricks and will see things correctly.

12. *Cleaning up for the night.* Wash out your brushes in warm, sudsy water, removing the masking tape first. Blot the brushes dry on paper towels and stand them upright in a container so they will dry overnight or dry them with a hair dryer. Scrub the paint off your stencils with plastic scouring pads under hot water. If the paint has dried, soak the stencils in hot water with detergent for an

6. The "Early American Fudge Factor" as seen in the Joshua Eaton House, Bradford, New Hampshire. When Moses Eaton stenciled this bedroom, he was not hampered by precise measuring; when he reached the corner, he added an extra swag and an extra leaf to finish the wall. Over the doorway he switched from the swag-and-bell frieze to a narrower horizontal border. Note that he used hearts as clappers for the bells in the frieze.

hour and then scrub again. Place clean stencils between layers of newspaper so they dry flat. Scrub the excess paint off your palettes and wash them off.

CUTTING A STENCIL FROM ANY PATTERN

You can take the designs for stencils from bed-spreads, wallpaper, Oriental rugs, club insignias, and monograms with our method. There is one big trick, however, because you can't cut a circle, it will fall out of your stencil. Even a long curved line is tricky.

The solution is to cut bridges in the line or circle, that is, cut it in two-inch segments separated by one-quarter-inch bridges (sections you don't cut). When you stencil, the eye will see an unbroken stenciled line.

CHECKLIST FOR CUTTING

Cutting a stencil should move along smartly; here is a checklist to help.

1. Hold the knife as you would a pencil but using a heavier pressure.
2. Move the stencil as you cut, sliding it one way and cutting long sweeping strokes the other way. If your stencil doesn't slide easily, find a harder surface to cut against.
3. Avoid short jagged cuts.
4. Make sure you use the *curved* side of the knife because that is the cutting edge.

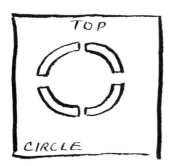

Cut bridges when cutting a circle

Chapter Five

CREATE A STENCILED ROOM

You've decided to stencil a room; it's much cheaper than wallpapering, and you can tailor the designs in this book to fit your walls. When you finish, the room will be a one-of-a-kind work of art—*your* work of art!

1. Select patterns and colors. You have already cut stencils and practiced stenciling as we suggested in chapter 4; now put your favorite patterns on paper and tape them up in the room you plan to stencil. Try different color combinations for the same pattern. *Live* with the designs and colors for several days to make sure that they feel right. If they don't, then this is the time to change your mind and make adjustments.

You can, of course, sketch the room on paper (include the windows, fireplace, and doors) and then rough in your patterns, but we find that actually taping up a few examples is a simpler and better way to select the final patterns and colors.

Start by choosing a frieze, the deep border that runs around the room just below the ceiling. Almost every room in a contemporary home can use this amount of color and pattern, even bathrooms. Select the window casing or doorway closest to the ceiling and measure the distance between it and the ceiling: this is your *limiting factor.* As most rooms have at least ten to twelve inches between the ceiling and the top of the woodwork, you will find that most of the period friezes in this book will fit your room.

If you need a narrower border, use a design designated a *horizontal border* at the ceiling or do what the early stencilers did: use a deep border everywhere except over the doors and windows, where they switched to a narrow one. See the photograph of the Joshua Eaton House on page 16.

Borders and friezes should be at least one inch from ceilings, doors, and moldings. Because your stencils include a one-inch border at the top and bottom, when you place them directly up against ceilings, doors, and moldings, your designs will be placed exactly and you will not have to measure.

a guide for the placement of stenciling

2. Prepare the walls. Paint the room with a *flat-finish* latex or oil paint. Stenciling will disguise small irregular bumps and cracks in the plaster, but large holes and cracks must first be filled in with spackle, then sanded smooth and painted before stenciling. You can even stencil on specially prepared textured paints, which will cover up imperfections in the wall surface.

Our patterns can be used against such background colors as gold, light yellow, pale greens and blues, and antique white. You will get an interesting contemporary effect by stenciling in white on top of a bright background, such as chartreuse. See stencil 65 for an example of stenciling in white on a blue background.

7. This contemporary bedroom in a house on Long Island shows the very beautiful effect that can be achieved with stenciling. *(Photograph by Arnold T. Rosenberg courtesy Thomas K. Woodard and Blanche Greenstein)*

If you are not going to repaint the room, be sure to wash the walls with soap and water to remove the dirt.

3. Tips for working easily and efficiently.

a) Start in an inconspicuous corner. Begin stenciling in a place that does not readily catch the eye, such as over the frame of the door people use to enter the room. Secure your stencil with two or three pieces of masking tape. Begin your stenciling with the predominant color first. When doing your frieze, follow the line of the ceiling, even if it is irregular or uneven. To keep brush marks off the ceiling, apply masking tape across the top of the stencil.

For vertical borders, you need a plumb line to indicate the true vertical; chalk in a long plumb line and then measure from it. The early stencilers placed vertical borders two feet apart and then put central units inside these panels about six to twelve inches apart.

b) As you work, put enough paint on your palette to be able to stencil several repeats of the design. Wipe your stencil clean with a soapy rag after four or five printings. Keep a wet rag handy in case you make a mistake. If you discover an accidental drip several hours after it has happened, use a little scouring powder to rub it off.

The total time of pounding with your brushes before the paint begins to dry on the bristles is approximately three

8. The white stenciling on a chartreuse background imparts a fresh, modern feeling to an early American frieze in this Meadowbrook, Pennsylvania, dining room.

to four hours; by then your arm will begin to ache. It's time to wash the brushes in hot soapy water.

If you stop for a cup of coffee or to answer the phone, wrap your brushes in damp rags or put them in plastic bags in the refrigerator to keep the fast-drying paint from hardening.

c) We stencil about three or four hours and then stop. Our eyes and minds, arms and backs give out if we work any longer.

Remember to clean up carefully, as we suggested in chapter 4. If your stencil becomes badly wrinkled, put it in very hot water to soften it and then press out the creases with your hand.

When you begin stenciling again, be sure your brushes are completely dry. Otherwise, moisture in the bristles will dilute the paint.

d) Let the paint set for at least a month before washing off a stray fingerprint. Manufacturers suggest not washing latex for at least three weeks, giving it time to "cure" to a permanent hardness.

4. Ideas for specific areas and problem spots.

► A "chopped-up" room (one with many windows and doors) can be tied together by stenciling a continuous frieze around all the walls.

► High ceilings can be lowered optically by stenciling a deep frieze around the room. You can also paint a deep border below the ceiling—perhaps at thirteen inches—and then stencil a frieze on top of the border.

► A dreary stairwell in an old school was brightened by stenciling big bold flowers on the walls.

► An attic bedroom was livened up by a twelve-year-old girl when she designed and stenciled a border of pink flowers around the ceiling.

9. Kitchen window, Huntingdon Valley, Pennsylvania. The simple leafy border nicely finishes a hard-to-decorate area.

Chapter Six

STENCIL BEDSPREADS, CURTAINS, AND OTHER FABRICS

Enhance your stenciled walls by stenciling white muslin curtains with the same border or using the patterns on a dust ruffle or a coverlet in a bedroom or even on window shades. Stenciling fabric is easy if you follow our simple directions.

1. Selecting fabric. You can stencil almost any fabric, including all natural fiber materials such as cotton, linen, denim, silk, or muslin. Do not choose any fuzzy fabrics with a deep nap, because too much paint is needed to cover and penetrate the fabric. Do not stencil any fabrics labeled

10. The Stenciled Bedroom in The American Museum in Britain, Bath, England. This small bedroom is from the Joshua La Salle House, built around 1830 in Windham, Connecticut. The stenciling on boards on the far wall suggests wallpaper designs of the period. The wonderful stenciled coverlet is from New Jersey. *(Photograph courtesy The American Museum in Britain)*

Dry Clean Only, because acrylic paints will not withstand frequent dry cleaning.

Stencil a trial pattern on a scrap of fabric or along an inside seam to see how the fabric takes the stencil and how the colors work.

2. Preparing fabric. No matter what material you choose, even ready-made curtains and sheets, wash it first to remove the sizing. Manufacturers treat all fabrics with sizing to stiffen them, and if it is not washed out with soap and water, the stenciling will not adhere properly. Remove all wrinkles by ironing the material.

3. Getting ready to stencil. The material should be stretched as taut as possible, so you can paint without wrinkling it or distorting the design. First, cover your work surface with newspaper and then spread over it a layer of paper toweling or a sheet of white blotter. Tack your fabric so it will not move or tape it with masking tape. Mark guidelines for placing your design with tailor's chalk or faint pencil lines.

4. Fabric paints. Use the very same paints you use on your walls to stencil fabric. Acrylic and latex paints are permanent once they dry and can be washed over and over. Our favorites are acrylic paints in tubes or plastic jars. Try acrylic *fabric paints* or textile screen-printing inks that dry permanently and wash up with soap and water. We recom-

mend mixing them with a *matte medium,* which extends the paint so it works down into the fibers. A matte medium is a thick white substance that resembles glue and does not dilute the color.

We recommend stenciling thin layers of paint into the fabric; it is much better to apply two, three, or even four thin coats than one thick coat, which will stiffen the fabric and crack.

5. Stenciling fabric. Stenciling fabric is similar to stenciling walls. The most important thing is to have practically *no* paint on your brush; pounce it on newspaper until it is practically dry. As you stencil, pound the paint down into the fibers of the fabric; do not simply cover the fabric surface.

Allow the first stenciled area to dry thoroughly before applying the second stencil. When your design is finished, let the fabric dry for twenty-four hours, and do not wash it for a week, and then only with a mild soap.

6. Setting the color. Follow the manufacturer's directions if you are using acrylic fabric paints. For most acrylic fabrics it is not necessary to set the color.

If you wish to set the stencil by ironing it, place a dry cloth over the design and iron for two to three minutes at medium heat. Repeat on the back side. Do not use a steam iron. For synthetic fabrics such as rayon and nylon set the iron at the lowest temperature and press for ten minutes.

Chapter Seven

A GALLERY OF STENCIL DESIGNS

We have grouped the full-size patterns illustrated according to the buildings and rooms where they were found. A short preface introduces and identifies each group.

Originally, many of the patterns were done in green and red, a very common color scheme used in early American stenciling. We show some patterns in the original colors and other patterns in more contemporary color schemes. We state the original colors for the stencils in each preface.

Each room contains some of the original stencil elements: central units, horizontal and vertical borders, and friezes. You may use all or some of the elements of a room, or combine patterns from different houses. However, as each stenciler had his own style, the designs that are illustrated together complement each other.

We traced the original patterns, made stencils from them, and stenciled them on special paper for reproduction in this book to give you the exact texture and "feel" of early American work.

Each pattern is identified by its form and by the location where it was found—that is, the historic name of the building (not the name of the present owners) and the geographic location.

We do not know the identity of any of the stencilers of these patterns except for Moses Eaton, Jr. Because his stencil case containing seventy-eight stencils has been found, his patterns can be identified by matching each stencil against the painted design.

In only two houses were we sure the stenciling was Moses Eaton's. One was the Stephen Damon House in Amherst, New Hampshire, where we could be sure it was Eaton's work because we found in his kit every one of the patterns used there. The other was the David Thompson House, now demolished; two stenciled walls from this house are in the Brick Store Museum in Kennebunk, Maine, and they have been positively identified as Eaton's work.

There is a possibility that Eaton stenciled the Tobias Ricker House in Buckfield, Maine, working with Rufus Porter. In other houses we found Eaton-like patterns mixed with patterns that were not in his kit; so we are chary of saying it is Eaton's work.

We have dated the stenciling where possible, but in most cases it is difficult to be specific. The patterns date from about 1800 to about 1840.

Section 1   JOSIAH SAGE HOUSE, SOUTH SANDISFIELD, MASSACHUSETTS

When the stenciler first came to this elegant white frame house in the Berkshire Hills in southwest Massachusetts, he put a sampler of his designs on a wall in the attic. The householders commissioned him to stencil five rooms, and his repertoire proved to be far richer than what is seen in the sampler. The Sage house has some of the loveliest and most sophisticated stenciling we have seen.

The sampler was done around a fanlight window, as seen in the photograph, and was crudely stenciled in only one color, a blackish olive. The date 1824 is scratched above the window, but it may not be the date of the stenciling. In this book we have stenciled some of the designs from the sampler in hot pink and lime green, a color scheme that would work well in a little girl's room or nursery. These designs do not appear elsewhere in the house.

In the rooms downstairs the stenciling was done in yellow-green, tomato red, white, and ochre on a gray ground; we suspect that the yellow-green was once a deeper green that has faded over the years. We used approximately the original colors to stencil vertical borders, a central

motif, and a delicate frieze or baseboard design. Note the white overlay in the vertical diamond pattern; you make this by cutting a third stencil and stenciling the white over the green diamond. We have stenciled other patterns in dusty rose and chocolate brown, a color scheme that was used in a Florida bedroom to coordinate with a handmade quilt.

We found the patterns from the Josiah Sage House repeated approximately twenty miles away in an old inn in Southwick, Massachusetts, which is now a used-furniture shop. The rooms in the building had been painted, but we discovered the designs in a small windowless room, probably a closet, at the top of the stairs. Many of the same motifs have been found in western New York near Rochester, roughly 250 miles away.

A crude imitation of one border from the sampler, the star flower and sideways heart design, has been found more than 600 miles away from South Sandisfield in McConnelsville, Ohio, in an old inn about 20 miles south of Zanesville.

Stencil 1. A central unit from the attic sampler.

Stencil 2. A central unit from the attic sampler.
The original had an empty space in the middle as shown here; you may want to add the heart
from the preceding pattern.

Stencil 3. *Above:* This central unit is an early American version of an ancient symbol of good fortune: the swastika. *Below:* A horizontal border, which may also be used as a frieze.

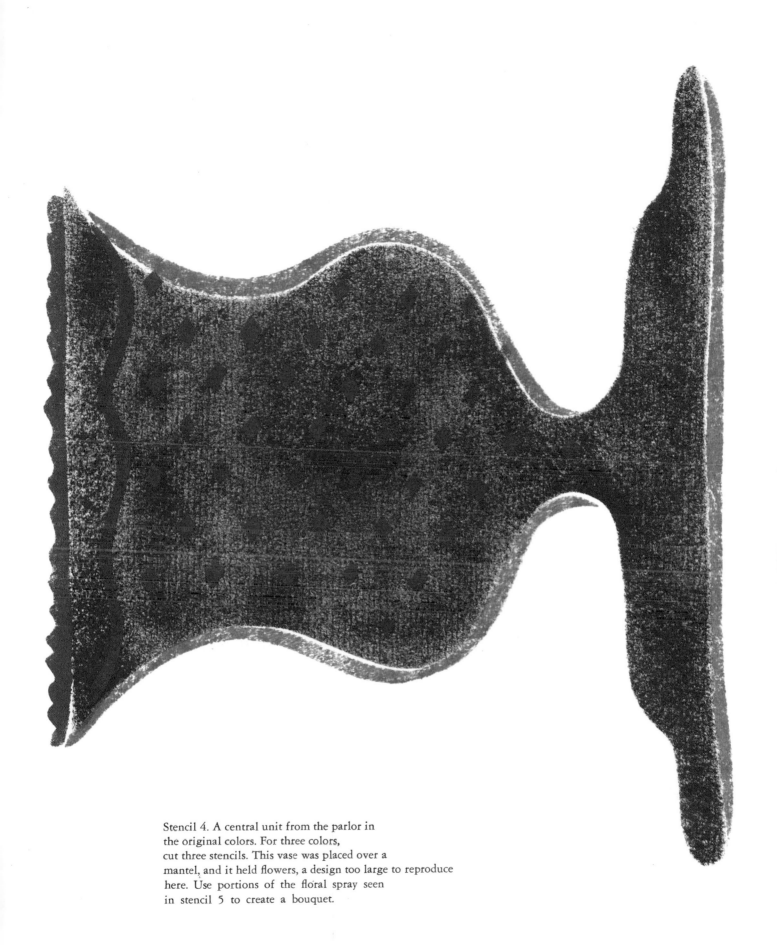

Stencil 4. A central unit from the parlor in
the original colors. For three colors,
cut three stencils. This vase was placed over a
mantel, and it held flowers, a design too large to reproduce
here. Use portions of the floral spray seen
in stencil 5 to create a bouquet.

Stencil 5. A central unit from the parlor in the original colors.
The gray elements show where the two sections of the pattern
overlap. Cut two pieces of vinyl 12″ by 13″ for your green and
red stencils. Trace the green design on the right-hand
page in solid lines and the gray areas in dotted lines. Then,
on the left-hand page, overlap the dotted lines and
trace the complete pattern in solid lines.

28

Stencil 6. Vertical borders from the parlor
in the original colors. For the overlay
on the diamond cut a third stencil
and stencil in white.

Stencil 7. A horizontal border from the parlor
in the original colors. It may also be used as a frieze.

Stencil 8. A vertical border from the bedroom. The gray area shows the pattern overlap. Cut two pieces of vinyl 8″ by 22″. Begin by tracing the top brown leaves and stem on the left-hand page at the top of your brown stencil; then trace the gray areas in dotted lines. Next, move to the right-hand page, overlap the dotted-gray leaf and stem, and trace the pattern in solid lines. On your pink stencil with the berries remember to trace the vine to act as register marks. This delicate vine with berries was used to outline panels, and it also twined around windows.

Stencil 9. A central unit from the upstairs bedroom, which was also used in the parlor. The center could be rendered in a third color.

Stencil 10. A central unit from the bedroom, which was also used in the parlor.

Section 2

HALL TAVERN, HISTORIC DEERFIELD, DEERFIELD, MASSACHUSETTS

These designs are from the ballroom in the Hall Tavern at Historic Deerfield in northern Massachusetts, where some of the stenciling is original and the rest has been carefully restored. The ballroom has gold walls and the patterns were done in green and red. We show them here in dusty blue and ming green. The Hall Tavern was moved from Charlemont, which is about fifteen miles west of Deerfield.

One wall is not original to the tavern, but is reproduced from a house from Colrain, which is about ten miles south of Deerfield. This wall has an unusual pattern of a horse and rider, which we show in black as a silhouette. The original color was blue-black.

Another unusual pattern we found here was a pomegranate-and-leaf border; the fruit was originally red. We have not found this motif elsewhere.

These blue and green designs could be used to decorate a bedroom or used as individual units to adorn a coverlet or pillows.

11. Ballroom in the Hall Tavern, Deerfield, Massachusetts. (*Photograph courtesy Historic Deerfield, Inc.*)

Stencil 11. A central unit from the ballroom.

Stencil 12. A horizontal border from the ballroom.

Stencil 13. A central unit from the ballroom.

Stencil 14. A central unit from the ballroom.

Stencil 15. A central unit on a wall that was originally in a house in Colrain, Massachusetts, which is now installed in the ballroom of the Hall Tavern.

Section 3

PETER FARNUM HOMESTEAD, FRANCESTOWN, NEW HAMPSHIRE

When we saw the Peter Farnum Homestead in the White Mountains of southern New Hampshire, it was being extensively restored by its owners. The original ochre walls of the parlor had been darkened by years of smoke from the fireplace and the stenciling had been dulled, but some of the molding had been removed and behind it we saw the bright original colors. The colors were aquamarine, rose, and dark blue, a color that was rarely used in the days of the early stencilers because blue pigment was expensive.

The artist had stenciled the parlor to appear as if it had been hung with formal imported wallpaper. He used intricate designs, tiny bows, and lacy intertwining borders; we present these patterns in their original colors.

The stenciler often added a special motif in the corners;

where the chair rail met the door molding, he used the quarter-fan pattern seen in stencil 16. We have found some of the same elements of this stenciling in other homes in the Francestown area.

Don't avoid the spiral-and-bow design because of the small dots. They are easy to cut, once you master the method we describe in the introductory text. This design was used in vertical rows approximately three feet apart around the room perhaps to suggest columns.

The narrower vertical borders would be interesting following the line of tile in your powder room, on a mirror frame, or to outline a window. Substitute the colors of your bathroom tile for these colors, or try white stenciling on a dark background.

Stencil 16. A quarter fan used
at the corners in the parlor
in the original colors.

Stencil 17. A central unit from the parlor in the original color.

Stencil 18. A vertical border
from the parlor in the original colors:
spiral with rose bows.
The rose is applied as an overlay.

Section 4

FRANKLIN PIERCE HOMESTEAD, HILLSBORO, NEW HAMPSHIRE

The artist who stenciled the home of the nation's fourteenth president used a type of stenciling entirely different from the single-motif repeat patterns. He used small delicate borders around doors, windows, moldings, and often close to ceilings and left the center of the walls free of design. He probably worked in this house before 1822, because some of the stenciling had been covered by a hand-blocked wallpaper that had been printed in 1822.

This work is attributed to the "border stenciler," and may be earlier than the single-motif repeat-pattern style. It is very similar to stenciling found nearby in Francestown and Peterborough. We suspect that the border stenciler traveled into Maine, because we found the same color scheme and patterns used in Hillsboro repeated in a small dressing room in the Taylor-Barry House in Kennebunk, Maine (see Section 8).

Franklin Pierce's father, Benjamin, built the homestead in 1804 and the family moved in that year, shortly after Franklin's birth. Benjamin Pierce served as a general in the American Revolution and was elected to two terms as governor of New Hampshire. He loved to entertain at parties, open houses, dances, and quilting and spelling bees, and he loved the holiday season of Christmas, to which he always gave extra celebration because it was also his birthday. Family tradition says that he personally chose the frieze stenciled in his ballroom, which is included here with the Taylor-Barry House. It was called "Christmas holly, bent pine and lighted candles."

The patterns in the Pierce Homestead are faded now and most of the stenciling has been painted over. We illustrate a frieze and three borders in moss green and Colonial red, and note the original colors with each pattern.

Stencil 19. A frieze from the dressing room off the north bedroom, originally stenciled in blue-black on a pink ground.

Stencil 20. A border from the north bedroom.
This design outlines doors, windows, baseboards, and the ceiling,
and appears in blue-black on ochre. If you use a second
color, as in the lower version, you will emphasize
the border's undulating effect.

Section 5

KENNETH LEARY HOUSE, FARMINGTON, NEW HAMPSHIRE

The bird on a branch, the starburst, the heartburst, and the other unusual designs in this section were found in the long-vacant Kenneth Leary House, which was falling into disrepair. The house was in Farmington, New Hampshire, located in the southwest corner of the state, about twenty-five miles from the Atlantic Ocean.

The original designs were done in green and red. We show them here in tangerine and seafoam green, a color combination that would look well in a plant room or sun porch. You can use either frieze and alternate the parrot-like bird with the heart and flower central units.

Stencil 21. A pinwheel central unit.

Stencil 22. A starburst central unit.

Stencil 23. For this delicate swag-and-tassel frieze cut one piece of vinyl 17″ by 10″.

Stencil 24. A frieze that can be used either up or down;
in the original stencil the major element appears as an arch.

54

Stencil 23. A horizontal leaf border.

Stencil 26. A central unit: the bird on the opposite page sits on this leafy branch. Cut the branch stencil on a piece of vinyl 11″ by 7″ and be sure to trace the gray area in dotted lines as register marks to help place the bird. Next, cut the bird on two stencils, putting the body on the first stencil with register marks to place it on the branch; then cutting the feet, wing, and eye on the second stencil.

Stencil 27. A heartburst central unit.

Section 6

STEPHEN DAMON HOUSE, AMHERST, NEW HAMPSHIRE

It was in this elegant old farmhouse, off a country road in southern New Hampshire, that we saw our first early American wall stenciling—a bedroom with a basket of strawberries centered over a mantel and strawberry vines climbing along the molding. This bedroom was stenciled for Stephen Damon and his wife, Nancy, by Moses Eaton, Jr., the best known and most prolific of the early stencilers.

Damon built the house in 1815 on land his father had

given him. In the north chamber on the second floor Eaton covered the walls with a raspberry wash and did his designs in green and red. Between the two front windows he stenciled a single willow tree, the Colonial symbol of immortality, thus wishing a long life to the couple.

The patterns are shown in their original colors. This is the only place we have found the basket of strawberries.

If you wish to use a willow, you can find it in stencil 36.

Stencil 28. A horizontal border in the original colors.
This strawberry vine ran around the baseboard in the bedroom.

Stencil 29. A central unit in the original colors.

Stencil 30. A basket-of-strawberries central unit
in the original colors. The gray area indicates
the pattern overlap. Cut two pieces of vinyl 12″ by 12″.
On your first stencil trace the basket's red areas
in solid lines and the gray areas in dotted lines; then
move to the right-hand page and complete the red
part of the design. Repeat this process for the green
areas on the second stencil.

63

Stencil 31. A central unit in the original colors.

Stencil 32. A vertical border
in the original color.
This simple border, which we call
the diamond-and-leaf border,
was one of Eaton's favorites.
He used it to outline the architectural
features in a room, and
he usually used it vertically.

MID-EIGHTEENTH-CENTURY FARMHOUSE, DANVILLE, NEW HAMPSHIRE

The stenciling in this large farmhouse on a twisting country lane in southeast New Hampshire had been hidden by layers of wallpaper until it was discovered in the mid-1950s by a new owner.

Three rooms had been stenciled, and the patterns are shown here. The front hall was painted gray and stenciled in green and red; the patterns are illustrated here in creamy apricot and light brown. The parlor was painted ochre and stenciled in green and red; we show the patterns in dusty rose and garnet red. A bedroom was painted with a raspberry wash and stenciled in green and red; the patterns are seen here in the original colors. Two willows were stenciled over a mantel, and they alternated with baskets of flowers.

Stencil 33. A central unit from the hall.
This oak-leaf motif would also be effective used
as a frieze near the ceiling.

Stencil 34. A formal frieze from the parlor.
The heart is an overlay, so stencil the pink areas first.
Leave enough space at the top of your wall for the dark red stripes.

Stencil 35. A frieze from the hall.

Stencil 36. A central unit from the bedroom in the original color.
Trace this large willow on one piece of vinyl 12″ by 13″.
The gray areas indicate the pattern overlap.

Stencil 37. A central unit from the bedroom
in the original colors. This basket of
flowers was a favorite Moses Eaton pattern.
He used it often, alternating it
with a willow tree. Cut two pieces of vinyl
12″ by 12″. The gray areas indicate
the pattern overlap.

Stencil 38. Two horizontal borders.

Section 8

TAYLOR-BARRY HOUSE, KENNEBUNK, MAINE

The patterns in the Taylor-Barry House in Kennebunk near the Maine coast represent a type of stenciling entirely different from the single-motif repeat patterns. This stenciling features a border that is used both horizontally and vertically, and this type of stenciling may well be earlier in date than the other patterns we show. The Taylor-Barry patterns are given in their original colors.

Both the lower and upper halls in the house have raspberry-pink walls with a black stenciled border on a narrow white background. The stenciler of the border used quarter fans in the corners over the chair rails. The fans echoed the fanlights over the doors in the house.

We found these same patterns in a very faded condition in the Franklin Pierce Homestead in Hillsboro, New Hampshire, and in Peterborough, New Hampshire. They will enhance any room, particularly an entrance hall or a dining room.

Exterior Barry House
Kennebunk, Maine c. 1803

Front Hall border stenciling

Stencil 39. A border and a quarter fan in the original colors.

Stencil 40. A frieze in the original colors.

Section 9

DAVID THOMPSON HOUSE, KENNEBUNK, MAINE

The David Thompson House has been demolished, but two of its walls stenciled by Moses Eaton, Jr., are on display at the Brick Store Museum in Kennebunk, Maine, where we traced these patterns. They are shown in the original colors, an unusual color scheme of red, deep mulberry, and green. Eaton stenciled on gray walls, so the original is not so bright as our rendering on white.

Here also is Eaton's pineapple, which he stenciled frequently in Maine at a time when most people probably had never seen an actual pineapple, which was a Colonial symbol of hospitality. Eaton's handsome fruit welcomed visitors into the hallways and parlors of many rural homes.

Stencil 41. A central unit from Wall 1 in the original colors.

Stencil 42. A frieze from Wall 1: the oak leaf,
one of Eaton's favorite patterns in the original colors.

Stencil 43. A swag-and-leaf frieze in the original colors.
The gray areas indicate the pattern overlap.
Cut two pieces of vinyl 20″ by 8″.

Stencil 44. A central unit from Wall 2 in the original colors.

Stencil 45. A central unit from Wall 1 in the original colors.

Stencil 46. A central unit from Wall 2 in the original color.

Section 10

WATERMAN HOUSE, WALDOBORO, MAINE

This gracious white house, built in 1775 in a town a few miles from the Maine coast, once had stenciling in four rooms, but little of it remains today. A misguided tenant used scarlet paint over stencil patterns in a bedroom. The front hall escaped the repainting; we show two patterns that remain stenciled above a baseboard indicated in black.

The two patterns, a pineapple and a border, were originally stenciled in green and red on a gray wash. They are shown here in canary yellow and forest green, which works well against a black baseboard or a darker green one, if you wish. We show a baseboard in our rendering directly below the horizontal border with leaves and petite flowers that ran up a flight of stairs. This example also shows how to turn a corner.

Stencil 47. A pineapple central unit.
The gray areas indicate the pattern overlap.

Stencil 48. A border that runs
up a stairway over a baseboard shown
here in black. To continue the
pattern, repeat the two elements at
the top of the page where
the incline begins.

92

Section 11

TOBIAS RICKER HOUSE, BUCKFIELD, MAINE

In this simple farmhouse high on a hill in a rural town we discovered some of the most colorful and complicated stenciling we had yet seen. This included the use of four colors in a stencil: the four-color pineapple with ochre fruit, a touch of cadmium red on top, and leaves two shades of green—olive and a darker, bluer green. We also found free-hand painting and spongework under the stenciled willow trees.

The patterns were those of Moses Eaton, Jr., but they had been changed and elaborated. It is possible that the work was partly Eaton's and partly that of Rufus Porter, a mural painter and innovative artist who used the sponge-work technique. Porter worked with Eaton on a trip that took them from southwest New Hampshire north to Sebec, Maine, around 1824. It is possible that they worked together on this house since Sebec is about eighty miles northeast of Buckfield.

The patterns are illustrated in their original colors: red, greens, and gold.

12. Tobias Ricker House, Buckfield, Maine.
Early American stenciled pineapples were usually done in two colors, sometimes three.
Here Moses Eaton created a pineapple in four colors.

Stencil 49. A central unit: a four-color
pineapple in the original colors. The gray areas
indicate the pattern overlap.

Stencil 50. A central unit: a three-color basket of flowers in the original colors.
The gray areas indicate the pattern overlap. Cut three stencils:
stencil green first, then gold, and finally red.

Stencil 51. A central unit: an asymmetrical willow with a bird in the original colors. The gray areas indicate the pattern overlap. Cut the willow on a stencil 12″ by 12″. Cut the bird on a second stencil; then cut his wing, top crest, and eye on a third stencil.

Stencil 52. A central unit in the original color.

Stencil 53. A sunburst central unit in the original color.

WELCOME ROOD TAVERN AND J. W. HILL FARM, FOSTER, RHODE ISLAND

The town of Foster recently had a historic building survey, and much of its stenciling was recorded for the first time. These patterns are from two buildings from this area on the western edge of Rhode Island. Similar patterns have been found across the border in Connecticut.

The designs are simple, bold, and large, and were applied with untrained spontaneity. They were originally done in black and pink, and green and red; we show them here in red and blue, a good color scheme for a kitchen or a powder room with solid-color matching towels. The red tulip border is particularly unusual, and so is the frieze with the sunflowers.

Stencil 54. A central unit.

Stencil 55. A vertical border of tulips.

Stencil 56. Two horizontal borders. To stencil the red flower with a blue dot in the center, make sure your brush has scarcely any red paint on it and then pound it around the *edges* of the flower. Leave the inside center somewhat free of paint, with the rest of the flower shading into the center. Stencil the blue dot heavily to fill this space.
Don't worry if the center isn't completely filled in; the effect is airy and interesting.

Stencil 57. A frieze.

Section 13

BATTY-BARDEN HOUSE, SCITUATE, RHODE ISLAND

An unusual design, a duck sitting on a bit of water, was hidden for years under the wallpaper in this historic house until discovered by a new owner. It was used as a repeat design in a parlor frieze.

The stenciling in the house was originally green and red. Here the patterns are in brown and rust because they are so suitable for a man's den or a boy's room. The poppy pattern is also unique to this house, and the entire effect here in central Rhode Island is different from the stenciling found on the Rhode Island coast or on the western border.

The flowers were stenciled in solid red, but we have shown the effect of shaded stenciling. The outer edges are stenciled darkly, leaving the center practically white in order to give a three-dimensional quality.

Stencil 58. A frieze: this duck can also be used as a central unit.

Stencil 59. A central unit of poppies.

Stencil 60. A central unit.

SMITH-APPLEBY HOUSE, SMITHFIELD, RHODE ISLAND

The following patterns were traced from the walls of the Smith-Appleby House in Stillwater, a tiny village in the township of Smithfield, Rhode Island, seven miles northeast of Providence. The house is owned by the Historical Society of Smithfield.

The original colors were yellow-green and dull red on a pale gray ground. We illustrate the designs from the northwest parlor in true blue and sun yellow; another from the attic stairway is done in a lighter blue.

We have stenciled a frieze in white against a blue ground to show how the old patterns can be given a contemporary look.

Stencil 61. A central unit from the northwest parlor.

Stencil 62. A central unit from the northwest parlor.

Stencil 63. A bell-and-tassel frieze
from the northwest parlor. The gray areas
indicate the pattern overlap.
Cut two pieces of vinyl 20″ by 9″.

114

Stencil 64. The frieze from the attic stairway.

116

Stencil 65. The frieze from the attic stairway stenciled in white on a dark background to achieve a contemporary effect.

Stencil 66. Two vertical borders from the northwest parlor.

Stencil 67. A central unit from the northwest parlor.

Section 15

PATTERNS FROM TWO COVERLETS AND A TABLECLOTH

This section presents stencil designs from two coverlets, one from New England and one from central New York, and from a tablecloth from southeast Pennsylvania. Stenciled fabrics are hard to find today because of the fragility of the material.

The first group of patterns is from a floral-stenciled muslin coverlet made in New England about 1825 and now in the collection of the Museum of American Folk Art in New York City. The central design was too large for reproduction in this book; so we are illustrating some of the smaller patterns from the coverlet in their original colors.

The second set of patterns is from a fruit-and-flower decorated counterpane from Lisle, New York, which is in Broome County near Binghamton. It was made in 1831 by Lucinda Linnell Howland and is in the collection of the Cortland County Historical Society, Cortland, New York.

Mrs. Howland was a bride in 1831 when she decided to make the unbleached muslin coverlet; an unidentified neighbor decorated it for her. The artist stenciled some designs, including pears, lemons, cherries, and apples and also worked freehand. The paint was applied thickly in spots and is developing small cracks.

The third collection of patterns is from a homespun tablecloth made in Chester County in southeast Pennsylvania in the mid-1800s. We show a flower basket that was stenciled in each of the four corners and two butterflies. These designs are in the original colors. The tablecloth is in the collection of Patricia Brown Schad.

If you wish to use these designs, refer to chapter 6, on stenciling fabric, for detailed directions. Because these designs are much smaller and more intricate to cut than wall patterns it would be wise to have considerable wall-stenciling experience before attempting them.

Stencil 68. Floral coverlet: A central unit in the original colors.

Stencils 69 and 70. Floral coverlet *above:* The border design for the coverlet in the original colors. Cut the green leaves on one long stencil and add the flowers singly.
Floral coverlet *below:* Four individual units in the original colors. Cut each one on a small stencil.

Stencil 71. Floral coverlet: A central unit in the original colors.

Stencil 72. Floral coverlet: A central unit in the original colors.

Stencil 73. Fruit-and-flower counterpane: An individual unit in the original colors.

Stencil 74. Fruit-and-flower counterpane: An individual unit in the original colors.

Stencils 75 and 76. Fruit-and-flower counterpane *above:* A section of the border design for the counterpane in the original colors. Fruit-and-flower counterpane *below:* Two individual units in the original colors.

Stencil 77. Fruit-and-flower counterpane:
Two individual units in the original colors.

130

Stencil 78. Baskets-and-butterflies
tablecloth: Corner motifs in
the original colors. This basket
appears in each of the four corners
of the tablecloth, and the baskets
are joined by flowing ribbons,
butterflies, and flowers.

Stencil 79. Baskets-and-butterflies tablecloth:
Individual units in the original colors.
These butterflies were placed randomly over
the baskets and flowers.

SUGGESTIONS FOR ALTERNATIVE COLOR SCHEMES

There is nothing sacred about the color schemes in which we show the stencil patterns illustrated in this book; with entirely different colors they can effectively adapt themselves to contemporary tastes or to your present furnishings. Here are some additional color choices to help spark your ideas.

Remember, you will get a quite different effect if you stencil in white on a dark background.

Always feel free to experiment with your own colors and contribute your own ideas to this wonderfully decorative folk art.

Chapter Eight

FOLLOWING THE TRAIL
OF THE JOURNEYMAN STENCILER

Following the trail of the journeyman stenciler has been a fascinating task. We have traveled off the beaten track, down many dirt roads, and were welcomed by the proud owners of lovely old homes who treasure the unique art form preserved on their walls.

Alas, many early patterns have disappeared because of the fading, the scrubbing, and the repainting of the walls, or destruction of the house itself. However, there are places open to the public where you can see original work as well as reproductions and other places that have collections of tracings of old patterns. We include their addresses so you can write for specific information about their hours or to make special visiting arrangements. We welcome contributions to these lists.

MUSEUMS AND HISTORIC RESTORATIONS

The Brick Store Museum. 117 Main Street, Kennebunk, Maine 04043. This museum has two Moses Eaton panels and other fine stenciling in its Taylor-Barry House (see stencils 39 and 40).

Bump Tavern. Part of the Farmers' Museum of the New York State Historical Association, Lake Road, Cooperstown, New York 13326. In this turnpike tavern, originally located in Ashland, New York, there are five running feet of wall with original stenciling and the rest is restored.

The Doctor Hunt Office. North Street, Windham Center, Connecticut 06280. This one-room building was used as an office in the nineteenth century by a Doctor Hunt. It is now owned by the Windham Free Public Library, which will open it to anyone interested in seeing the stenciling. Contact the library, which is nearby, to make arrangements.

The Franklin Pierce Homestead. Hillsboro, New Hampshire 03244. This was the home of the nation's fourteenth president and of his father, Benjamin Pierce, who was governor of New Hampshire. It is closed during the winter. For information, write the New Hampshire Department of Resources and Economic Development, State House Annex, Concord, New Hampshire 03301. The stenciling here was done by a "border stenciler" (see stencils 19 and 20).

The Franklin Pierce Inn. U.S. Route 9, North Branch, Antrim, New Hampshire 03440. This inn is about five miles from the Franklin Pierce Homestead, and is still operating as an inn and restaurant. The stenciling in the Tap Room is original with some retouching, but the work may date later in the nineteenth century.

Genesee Country Museum. Mumford, New York 14511. Mailing address: P.O. Box 1819, Rochester, New York 14603. See the stenciling in the Peck-Jones Farmhouse, originally located in Phelps, New York. It is similar to the stenciling found nearby in LeRoy and East Bloomfield. The restoration is open daily from mid-May to mid-October and takes its name from the Genesee River.

Historic Deerfield. The Street, Deerfield, Massachusetts 01342. Visit the Hall Tavern, which has stenciling (see stencils 11-15).

Old Sturbridge Village. Sturbridge, Massachusetts 01566. See the stenciling in the Parsonage (Richardson House) and the Tavern in the Center Village section of this restoration.

Shelburne Museum. U.S. Route 7, Shelburne, Vermont 05482. This museum has two houses with stenciling, the Dutton House, which is from Vermont, where there are fragments of the original work and the remainder is restored, and the Stencil House, where the work is original. This house is originally from Columbus, Chenango County, central New York. In the winter the museum is open only by appointment.

The Smith-Appleby House. Stillwater Road, Smithfield, Rhode Island 02917. This house is owned by the Historical Society of Smithfield, a town situated seven miles northeast of Providence near Pawtucket. See stencils 61-67. The house is open to the public by special arrangement; telephone the Smithfield Town Clerk for help in contacting the Historical Society.

ORGANIZATIONS OWNING STENCIL PATTERNS

The Metropolitan Museum of Art. Fifth Avenue at 82nd Street, New York, New York 10028. The museum's Print Department has photocopies of the 2,000 stencils in the Janet Waring Collection.

Providence Preservation Society. 24 Meeting Street, Providence, Rhode Island 02903.

Rhode Island Historical Preservation Commission. 150 Benefit Street, Providence, Rhode Island 02903.

The Society for the Preservation of New England Antiquities. 141 Cambridge Street, Boston, Massachusetts 02114. The society has the original Janet Waring Collection of more than 2,000 wall and furniture stencils and a photocopied set of the stencils. The society also owns Moses Eaton's stencil kit, which is *not* on display.

NOTES

CHAPTER ONE

1. Jean Lipman and Alice Winchester, *The Flowering of American Folk Art 1776–1876* (New York: The Viking Press in Cooperation with the Whitney Museum of American Art, 1974), p. 6.

2. Interview, William R. Scott of William R. Scott, Inc., publishers, March 10, 1980.

3. Interview, Barbara Hunt Smith, Janet Waring's great-niece, February 21, 1980.

CHAPTER TWO

1. The scholar was Pierre Gélis-Didot. Janet Waring, *Early American Stencils on Walls and Furniture* (1937; reprint ed., New York: Dover Publications, 1968), p. 18.

2. Paul Lacroix, *Histoire de l'imprimerie* (Paris: Adolphe Delahays, Libraire, 1852), p. 57.

3. Thomas Williams and James Calvert, *Fiji and the Fijians* (New York: D. Appleton & Co., 1859), p. 51.

4. Frances Blakemore, *Japanese Design Through Textile Patterns* (New York: John Weatherhill, Inc., 1978). Also, "Exhibition of Traditional Japanese Designs: The Tom and Frances Blakemore Collection of Textiles, Stencils and Costumes," The Minneapolis Institute of Arts, Minneapolis, Minnesota, October 15, 1980–January 4, 1981.

5. Jane Barbour and Doig Simmonds, eds., *Adire Cloth in Nigeria* (Ibadan, Nigeria: The Institute of African Studies, University of Ibadan, 1971), p. 17.

6. The advertisement appeared in the *Federal Gazette* July 29, 1796. Alfred Coxe Prime, *The Arts and Crafts in Philadelphia, Maryland, and South Carolina, 1786–1800* (Topsfield, Mass.: The Wayside Press for the Walpole Society, 1932), p. 305.

7. Waring, *Early American Stencils,* p. 26.

8. Jean Lipman, *Rufus Porter, Yankee Pioneer* (New York: Clarkson N. Potter, 1968), pp. 5, 25.

9. Interview with Willard C. Richardson, Eaton's great grandson, October 8, 1979.

10. Letter to author, March 31, 1980.

11. Leigh Rehner Jones, "Nineteenth-Century Interior Decorative Wall Painting: A Four-County Central New York Overview—Otsego, Chenango, Cortland and Tompkins Counties" (Master's thesis, State University of New York College, Oneonta, 1979).

12. I. T. Frary, *Ohio in Homespun and Calico* (Richmond, Va.: Garrett and Massie, 1942), p. 75, pl. 19.

13. Dorothy H. Candage, *A Record of Early American Wall Stencils Found in Blue Hill, Maine, and Nearby* (published by the author, 1979), p. 2.

14. Lipman, *Rufus Porter,* p. 153.

15. *Ibid.*

16. Lipman and Winchester, *The Flowering of American Folk Art, 1776–1876,* p. 205.

17. Interview with Louisa Richardson Fairfield, Eaton's great granddaughter, October 4, 1979.

18. Waring, *Early American Stencils,* p. 57.

19. *Ibid.,* p. 26.

20. Interview with Willard C. Richardson, October 8, 1979.

21. *Ibid.*

22. Lipman, *Rufus Porter,* p. 129.

23. Quoted in Alfred Coxe Prime, *The Arts and Crafts in Philadelphia, Maryland, and South Carolina, 1721–1785* (Topsfield, Mass.: The Wayside Press for The Walpole Society, 1929), p. 276.

24. Richardson Wright, *Hawkers & Walkers in Early America* (Philadelphia: J.B. Lippincott, 1927), p. 56.

BIBLIOGRAPHY

ALLEN, EDWARD B. *Early American Wall Paintings 1710–1850*. 1926. Reprint. Watkins Glen, N.Y.: Century House, 1969.

BACON, RICHARD M. *The Art and Craft of Wall Stenciling*. New York: Funk & Wagnalls, 1977.

BARBOUR, JANE, and SIMMONDS, DOIG, eds. *Adire Cloth in Nigeria*. Ibadan, Nigeria: The Institute of African Studies, University of Ibadan, 1971.

BISHOP, ADELE, and LORD, CILE. *The Art of Decorative Stenciling*. New York: Penguin Books, 1978.

BLAKEMORE, FRANCES. *Japanese Design Through Textile Patterns*. New York: John Weatherhill, Inc., 1978.

BOTHWELL, DORR, and FREY, MARLYS. *Notan: The Dark-Light Principle of Design*. New York: Reinhold Book Corporation, 1968.

BRAZER, ESTHER STEVENS. *Early American Decoration*. Springfield, Mass.: The Pond-Ekberg Co., 1961.

CANDAGE, DOROTHY H. *A Record of Early American Wall Stencils Found in Blue Hill, Maine, and Nearby*. Blue Hill, Me.: The Mountain Press, published by the author, 1979.

CANDEE, RICHARD M. *Housepaints in Colonial America: Their Materials, Manufacture and Application*. New York: Chromatic Publishing Co., 1967.

————. "The Rediscovery of Milk-based House Paints and the Myth of 'Brickdust and Buttermilk' Paints." *Old-Time New England* (The Bulletin of The Society for the Preservation of New England Antiquities), 58 (July 1967–April 1968).

DOSSIE, ROBERT. *The Handmaid to the Arts*. London: A. Millar, W. Law, and R. Cater; New York: Wilson, Spence and Mawman, 1769.

FALES, DEAN A., JR. *American Painted Furniture 1660–1880*. New York: E.P. Dutton, 1972.

FRARY, I. T. *Ohio in Homespun and Calico*. Richmond, Va.: Garrett and Massie, 1942.

GÉLIS-DIDOT, PIERRE. *La peinture décorative en France du XVIe au XVIIIe siècle*. Paris: Librarie-Imprimeries Réunies, 1888–1890.

GOTTESMAN, RITA SUSSWEIN, comp. *The Arts and Crafts in New York, 1726–1776*. New York: The New-York Historical Society, 1938.

————. *The Arts and Crafts in New York, 1777–1799*. New York: The New-York Historical Society, 1948.

————. *The Arts and Crafts in New York, 1800–1804*. New York: The New-York Historical Society, 1965.

HAYWARD, WILLIAM WILLIS. *The History of Hancock, New Hampshire, 1764–1889*. Lowell, Mass.: Vox Populi Press, S.W. Huse Co., 1889.

HOWE, FLORENCE THOMPSON. "Three Stenciled Counterpanes." The Magazine *Antiques* (March 1940).

JEWETT, KENNETH E. "Moses Eaton and the Art of Stencilling." *New Hampshire Profiles*, 22, no. 1 (January 1973).

JONES, LEIGH REHNER. "Nineteenth-Century Interior Decorative Wall Painting: A Four-County Central New York Overview—Otsego, Chenango, Cortland and Tompkins Counties." Master's thesis, State University of New York College, Oneonta, Cooperstown Graduate Programs, 1979. On file at New York State Historical Association Library, Cooperstown.

KOCH, ROBERT. *Louis C. Tiffany, Rebel in Glass*. New York: Crown Publishers, 1965.

LACROIX, PAUL; FOURNIER, ÉDOUARD; and SERÉ, FERDINAND. *Histoire de l'imprimerie*. Paris: Adolphe Delahays, Libraire, 1852.

LIPMAN, JEAN. *American Folk Art in Wood, Metal and Stone*. New York: Dover Publications, 1972.

————. *American Folk Decoration*. New York: Oxford University Press, 1951.

————. *Rufus Porter, Yankee Pioneer*. New York: Clarkson N. Potter, 1968.

————, and WINCHESTER, ALICE. *The Flowering of American Folk Art 1776–1876*. New York: The Viking Press in Cooperation with the Whitney Museum of American Art, 1974.

LITTLE, NINA FLETCHER. *The Abby Aldrich Rockefeller Folk Art Collection*. Boston: Little, Brown, in association with Colonial Williamsburg, 1957.

————. *American Decorative Wall Painting 1700–1850*. New York: Dutton Paperbacks, 1972.

————. *Country Arts in Early American Homes*. New York: Dutton Paperbacks, 1975.

MEASE, JAMES. *The Picture of Philadelphia*. Philadelphia: B. & T. Kite, 1811.

One Thousand Valuable Secrets in the Elegant and Useful Arts. Philadelphia: B. Davies, 1795.

PRIME, ALFRED COXE. *The Arts and Crafts in Philadelphia, Maryland, and South Carolina 1721–1785.* Topsfield Mass.: The Wayside Press for the Walpole Society, 1929.

————. *The Arts and Crafts in Philadelphia, Maryland, and South Carolina 1786–1800.* Topsfield, Mass.: The Wayside Press for the Walpole Society, 1932.

RAWSON, MARION NICHOLL. *From Here to Yonder, Early Trails and Highway Life.* New York: E.P. Dutton, 1932.

SIEBER, ROY. *African Textiles and Decorative Arts.* New York: The Museum of Modern Art, 1972.

Valuable Secrets Concerning Arts and Trades. London, 1775; Norwich, Conn.: Thomas Hubbard, 1795.

Valuable Secrets Concerning Arts and Trades. Boston: J. Bumstead's Printing Office, 1798.

Valuable Secrets in Arts and Trades. London: J. Barker, c. 1795.

Valuable Secrets in Arts Trades &c. New York: Evert Duyckinck, 1809.

VON SUCK, MAJORIE W. "The Janet Waring Collection of Stencils." *Old-Time New England* (The Bulletin of The Society for the Preservation of New England Antiquities), 44 (Spring 1954).

"Wallpaper Before 1830." *Early American Life* (February 1980).

WARING, JANET. *Early American Stencils on Walls and Furniture.* New York: William R. Scott, 1937. Reprint. New York: Dover Publications, 1968.

————. *Early American Wall Stencils: Their Origin, History & Use.* Reprint of *Early American Stencils on Walls and Furniture, Part One.* New York: William R. Scott, 1942.

WILLIAMS, THOMAS, and CALVERT, JAMES. *Fiji and the Fijians.* New York: D. Appleton & Co., 1859.

WRIGHT, RICHARDSON. *Hawkers & Walkers in Early America.* Philadelphia: J.B. Lippincott, 1927.

AUTHORS' BIOGRAPHIES

As a project for the nation's Bicentennial, Alice Fjelstul and Pat Schad set out to study and learn stenciling in the early American manner. For several years they traced patterns from walls in New England and developed an easy method for applying the designs to walls and fabrics. During the Bicentennial celebration in 1976 in Philadelphia they dressed in Colonial garb and displayed these patterns and techniques with other craftsmen of the early American arts. Now they give slide lectures on stenciling, conduct workshops, and accept private commissions.

ALICE BANCROFT FJELSTUL is a graduate of Wheaton College with a major in the history of art and she studied at the Rhode Island School of Design and the Pennsylvania Academy. She worked in the art department of the Associated Press News Features in Manhattan and was one of the founders of the St. Croix Valley Art Center, Hudson, Wisconsin. Fjelstul specialized in teaching children's art classes and art enrichment programs in Hudson, and after her move to Pennsylvania, in the Meadowbrook area. Alice moved to Minneapolis, Minnesota, in 1981, where she now teaches stenciling and folk art.

PATRICIA BROWN SCHAD is a graduate of Bucknell University with a B.S. in biochemistry and holds an M.S. in education from Boston University. Her other interests include antiques, archaeology, golf, and platform tennis. She has done biochemical research, taught science, and studied design at Philadelphia College of Art. She lives with her family in Huntingdon Valley, Pennsylvania, and is an active member of the Pennsylvania Guild of Craftsmen.

BARBARA MARHOEFER had never stenciled before she began writing this book for Alice and Pat, so she learned their methods while writing them up. She is a graduate of Trinity College, Washington, D.C., and the Columbia University Graduate School of Journalism and has worked for three newspapers, the present one being *The New York Times* on a part-time basis. She was an instructor in the Journalism Department at Temple University for three years. Her first book was *Witches, Whales, Petticoats and Sails, 300 Years of Adventures and Misadventures in Long Island History* (1971). She lived in Jenkintown, Pennsylvania, and was a member of the Philadelphia Children's Reading Round Table. She now lives in Minneapolis, Minnesota.

INDEX

Page references for illustrations are in **boldface** type.

Baldwin, Irwin DeWitt, 11
Batty-Barden House (Scituate, R.I.), 107, **108–110**
"border stenciler," 46, **47–48**, 134
Stephen Damon House (Amherst, N.H.), 1, 23, 59, **60–65**
De Forest, J. H., 11
Joshua Eaton House (Bradford, N.H.), 2, 8, 16, 18
Eaton, Moses, Jr., 1, 2, 3, 7, 8, 9, 10, 11, 16, 23, 59, **60–65**, 75, 80, **81–88**, 93, **94–101**, 134
Eaton, Moses, Sr., 3, 8, 9, 11
Peter Farnum Homestead (Francestown, N.H.), 42, **43–45**
Gates, Erastus, 11
Gilbert, E. J., 11
Goodrich, Henry O., 11
Hall Tavern (Deerfield, Mass.), **36–41**, 134
Howland, Lucinda Linnell, 120, **126–130**
Joshua La Salle House (Windham, Conn.), 21
Kenneth Leary House (Farmington, N.H.), 49, **50–58**
"Leroy," 11
Mid-Eighteenth-Century Farmhouse (Danville, N.H.), 66, **67–76**
Parker, Nathaniel, 11
Franklin Pierce Homestead (Hillsboro, N.H.), 7, 46, **47–48**, 77, 134
Poor, Jonathan D., 11
Porter, Rufus, 7, 8, 9, 10, 11, 23, 93
Priest, William, 6, 11
Rice, Emery, 11
Richardson family, 9
Richardson House, 134
Tobias Ricker House (Buckfield, Me.), 9, 20, 23, **93–101**
Josiah Sage House (South Sandisfield, Mass.), 2, 8, 11, 23, **24–35**
Smith-Appleby House (Smithfield, R.I.), 111, **112–119**, 134
"Stimp," 11
Taylor-Barry House (Kennebunk, Me.), 7, 46, **77–79**, 134
David Thompson House (Kennebunk, Me.), 80, **81–88**
Waring, Janet, 3–4, 6, 9, 10
Waterman House (Waldoboro, Me.), 89, **90–92**
Welcome Rood Tavern and J. W. Hill Farm (Foster, R.I.), 102, **103–106**
Williams, Lydia Eldredge, 8, 11